The
Beautiful
Bride

The Beautiful Bride

Mitchell Behr

Illustrations by Michael Jurado

A PERIGEE BOOK

A Perigee Book
Published by The Berkley Publishing Group
A member of Penguin Putnam Inc.
200 Madison Avenue
New York, NY 10016

First edition: January 1998

Published simultaneously in Canada.

The Putnam Berkley World Wide Web site address is
http://www.berkley.com

Library of Congress Cataloging-in-Publication Data
Behr, Mitchell.
    The beautiful bride / Mitchell Behr ; illustrations by Michael
Jurado.—1st ed.
      p. cm.
    "A Perigee book."
    ISBN 0-399-52373-1
    1. Weddings—United States—Planning. 2. Wedding costume—United
States. 3. Bridal bouquets—United States. 4. Weddings—United
States—Equipment and supplies. I. Title.
HQ745.B44 1998
395.2'2—dc21   97-24291
                                                                     CIP

Printed in the United States of America

10 9 8 7 6 5 4 3 2 1

To my sister, Caryn, the first bride who had the confidence in me to help her create her wedding vision. And to Cristina, Rebecca, Jill, Abbey, Peggy, Alison, Amy, Julie, Cheryl, Teryl, Jennifer, Michelle, and the other beautiful women who have brought me into their families and have allowed me to share this amazing time in their lives.

Contents

Preface

Preparing brides for their weddings was not something I had given much thought to when I was attending beauty school. But around the time I was getting ready to graduate, I was faced with a challenge I couldn't resist: helping my own younger sister, Caryn, with her wedding.

She didn't actually ask for my help—she sort of dared me. I had gone with her and my mom to the store in Chicago where Caryn had picked out a style of dress for her bridesmaids, which was, frankly, awful. "You are not serious," I said incredulously as she showed me the dress. And with that, my sister, a grown woman, started crying in the store, and swearing at me. She said, "Well, if you think you can find something better, that all these girls of different sizes can wear, then you just go ahead and do it!"

All I need to hear is someone doubting that I can do anything, and whatever it is, it gets done. I told her, "Give me until tomorrow," and sure enough, I showed up the next day with five pale violet dresses that looked good on everyone, for under $150 apiece.

The next challenge was doing my sister's hair and makeup for the wedding day: She's a no-makeup, low-maintenance girl who has no interest in being high maintenance or looking that way.

Having survived the ultimate challenge of pleasing both my sister and my mother and having withstood the anxiety of helping my sister and her wedding party look perfect on that most important of days, I figured I could easily handle the same thing for other women; the pressure could never be greater than it had been for my debut.

And so, for the past five years—in addition to my beauty and fashion work for magazines and the hairstyling I do for women in the fashion industry and the fashion press—I've been helping brides put together their vision for how they want to look for their wedding.

I love weddings. One of the really unfortunate phenomena that's common to them is that women don't remember their weddings. I think that has a lot to do with trepidation about all the details, and not always being comfortable with the decisions that have been made—because they've been imposed by other people.

It's my hope that this book will help brides—and the people close to them, who are helping them make decisions—map out the beauty and style aspects of that very special day, and the days leading up to it, to take some of the anxiety out of the experience. It is designed to be used as a reference book in the same way a cookbook is used: You can flip through, select the wedding beauty-related subject you're interested in at that time, take note of all the various options and alternatives, and the "ingredients" necessary for each, and then follow the recipes.

There are ideas for traditional weddings and alternative

ones, ideas concerning fashion and beauty as well as sentiment and protocol. I cover a lot of ground, speaking to a variety of sensibilities. But as you read, keep this in mind: What's reflected here are my tastes and my opinions. And I have a lot of those, as I'm sure my mother and sister could tell you.

Acknowledgments

I've had so much fun writing this book. Thank you, Suzanne, for allowing me to go "bride crazy." Hal and Robbie, you've done so much more than any two agents should have to. Bob and David—Thank You! Sari, you are amazing. Robert, your support is invaluable. And to all my friends who have learned way too much about becoming a beautiful bride.

The
Beautiful
Bride

Introduction:
How to Use
The Beautiful Bride

So, you're getting married.

Where will the wedding be? When? How many people will you have? Are you going to wear your mother's dress? How many bridesmaids will you have—and will they all be wearing the same dress? How are you going to wear your hair?

Pop quiz? No, just a small taste of some of the questions you'll be facing—or you may already be facing—once you let people know you've gotten engaged.

There are a lot of variables for you to juggle concerning your wedding—and lots of variables you can't control: The weather might not cooperate, parents can misbehave, the caterer might be running late.

While *The Beautiful Bride* can't put any of those things under your control, or help you to choose a band or a catering hall, it can help you make sure you look the part of the beautiful bride. All you need to do is follow the advice and tips provided in each chapter.

You'll discover valuable secrets for everything from photography choices to dress shopping, from easy hair options to makeup clues. I cover everything from your headpiece to your shoes, from your groom's grooming to finding flattering dresses that enhance your bridesmaids' body shapes. Using *The Beautiful Bride*, you can learn how to prepare yourself and your wedding party for the big day in an easy-to-follow, step-by-step fashion. Think of it as a map that can guide you through your wedding and the planning of it, and help you to enjoy the experience along the way.

Mainly, *The Beautiful Bride* is designed to be an antidote to all the anxiety surrounding your beauty and style issues for that day. The book aims to provide brides with all or most of the questions they'll need to ask themselves, and a vast menu of possible answers, regarding wedding style. It should help you think through your options before you get started and bolster your confidence in your own personal style, so that you can incorporate it as you plan and design your wedding.

I feel very strongly about brides being very personally involved in setting the tone for their weddings and making taste decisions themselves—even if they're the complete opposite of my taste. In fact, one of the brides I worked with, Christina, planned to have a totally mod wedding, making lots of style choices I personally didn't agree with. I voiced my opinions about what I thought was more stylish and appropriate, but after listening, Christina stuck to her guns. She wore a very sleek dress, held the wedding in a very minimal loft in Manhattan, and chose a very current band. In the end, I was pleasantly surprised to see that it all worked. She had coordinated everything, from the flowers to the food, to fit her concept, and it was beautiful. So, now, more than ever, I support the idea of brides being the architects of their wedding dream, whatever it is.

But beyond helpful hints and confidence boosting, in *The Beautiful Bride* you'll also probably discover alternatives and newsy tidbits about customs and fashion and beauty you never knew before—like the fact that it's a southern custom to make bridesmaids wear eye shadow that matches the color of the punch at the wedding; and that the reason most eye shadow (of any color) doesn't stay put is that most women don't realize they have to wear foundation underneath. (Powder by itself doesn't stick to skin.)

Feel free to skip from chapter to chapter. This is meant to be used as a reference book, which means you can jump around from one self-contained topic to another, depending on your needs. But more than anything, relax, and enjoy the process. This is going to be fun. . . .

Let's Get Started . . .
Developing Your
Wedding Vision

1

OFTEN, BRIDES I'VE WORKED WITH WILL RETURN TO my chair at the salon for a haircut a little while after the wedding and the honeymoon have taken place, and they'll bring me some of their wedding pictures, either to ask my advice about what to put in their wedding album, or just for fun. And that's when I get to see what happened at the wedding after I finished helping the bride get ready, put on her veil and took my exit.

Unfortunately, too often, a bride will sit down in that chair and begin to explain that she missed so much of her own wedding—either because her mother had it choreographed so that nearly every moment was spent with the photographer, or she was too nervous and wound up to be able to experience the day to the fullest. My reaction is always the same: "That's what happens when you are not totally involved in the orchestration of your own wedding, and not relaxed and comfortable! You might as well have eloped."

The very first thing that you need to decide is whose wedding it's going to be, and how much responsibility you want. Who is going to set the tone, for the style and beauty, and decide things like whether the wedding is formal or informal, indoors or outdoors? You? You and your fiancé? Your mother? Your family? I vote for you. The ideal is to set your own tone for the wedding but have help in achieving it, so that you can really be a guest at your own wedding when that day arrives and enjoy and remember it always.

If you're including other people in the decision-making process, be prepared to stand up for what you want. You want your friends and family to recognize you in your wedding. Sometimes, friends of a bride will tell me later on that the bride seemed really uncomfortable—as if she was a prop in a play. That's a scenario I find really upsetting. So much time goes into planning your wedding; to think it out and make sure your own sensibilities are represented will make you so much more proud and confident when the big day arrives.

Whatever role you're going to play, it's helpful if early on in your engagement, you sit down and write a paragraph or two about what you want your wedding to look like. Write it for yourself, so that you can get in touch with your own vision, and for the people whom you're going to involve in planning the wedding, so they know what's important to you. Describe the concept of the wedding you think you want. The more thought you give to your wedding in the beginning, the easier things will flow and the fewer headaches you'll incur. You might find it helpful to browse through some bridal magazines—particularly British and Australian ones because those tend to be the most beautiful— for some inspiration before sitting down to write.

Turn to these magazines to cull inspiring bridal beauty and style ideas:

Brides

British editions of *Brides* and *Modern Bride* (available at specialty newsstands)

Allure (for current hair and makeup tips)

Martha Stewart Bride

Martha Stewart Living (for personal flowers)

In your little composition to yourself, consider the first questions people will ask you. These are also the questions that are most important for you to address first:

- When are you going to get married? During what season will your wedding take place, and how much time will you need to prepare?

  The timing of the wedding can be affected by lots of things—like how long it might take you to save for the event if you're throwing it yourself. Or, if you want to wear your naturally curly hair straight for the wedding, the much-favored but humid month of June might not be such a good idea.

- How much can you, or whoever is paying for it, spend on the affair?

- How many people do you intend to invite?

- How formal is the affair going to be?

It's important to decide fairly quickly whether you want your wedding to be *formal* or *informal*, because this determines a lot of the style choices. You wouldn't wear the same type of dress for a Saturday night formal black-tie wedding as you might for a Sunday afternoon informal wedding. Of course, there are elements of a formal wedding that can be worked into an informal one—and a less formal wedding can still be elegant and sophisticated. But it's good to know early on what direction you're going in. In making this choice, think about your families—yours and your fiancé's. How formal are they, and what do they expect of you? It's important to figure out what everyone will be most comfortable with. And once you decide, you want to be consistent. You don't want to have the whole wedding party in simple, classic pearls except one bridesmaid who's wearing eclectic colored beads.

Sophisticated hair and an elegant,
flowing gown are the keynotes of
the formal bride.

The perfect attire for the informal
bride . . . a simple yet elegant
sheath dress.

Once you've determined those factors, you can move on to the next question that tops every busybody's list:

➤ What kind of dress are you going to wear?

Will you wear your mother's or grandmother's dress? Will you take apart a vintage wedding gown and combine parts of it with a modern design from Vogue patterns? Do you hate lacy, frilly dresses and love simple, modern styling? Or have you always envisioned yourself in a Victorian gown? There's a whole chapter devoted to selecting your dress in *The Beautiful Bride*. You'll want to assess your body, for better or worse, and have at least a rough idea of what you want to look like before you subject yourself to the ladies in your local bridal shop, or the scrutiny of family and friends.

The dress is a crucial element because it sets the tone for much of the rest of the wedding, not to mention the rest of your appearance.

➤ How will you wear your hair?

➤ What do you want your makeup and accessorizing to be like?

If you're a woman who wears no makeup and no jewelry, you need to think about what degree of makeup and accessorizing you'll realistically be comfortable with on your wedding day. You need to consider your own style in putting yourself together for your wedding day so that you don't feel as if you're wearing a costume in a play. Yet you need to remember that this day is being documented in photographs, which require more makeup than you may be accustomed to.

The next questions to address in your paragraph include:

❧ What kinds of flowers do you prefer, and how much can you spend on them?

This decision will be affected by the season during which your wedding is held. What do you want your personal flowers to look like? And can you do the flowers yourself? I recommend coordinating all the flowers in the wedding in one color scheme, from the ceremony to the reception, from the groom's family's personal flowers to the bride's. I find that this sort of continuity lends a certain sense of sophistication to the affair.

❧ How many bridesmaids will you have? And will they all be wearing the same dress?

❧ What sort of suit or tuxedo do you envision your fiancé and his attendants in? Don't be intimidated by your own initiative: Your paragraph isn't written in stone. You can change things. There are chapters here devoted to each of these topics that are designed to help you make informed choices.

Being aware of your own sensibilities will help you make the most of *The Beautiful Bride*, and ultimately plan your dream wedding, either by yourself or with family and friends.

Above all, keep in mind that your wedding day sets the tone for your family and your marriage. Be a little selfish. Your wedding sends a clear message about what type of couple you're going to be. That one brief day really does define who you are for the first time as an adult, married person.

Your Wedding Dress . . . The Ultimate Expression of Your Personal Style

2

O F ALL THE GARMENTS A WOMAN WILL EVER PUR-chase in her life, the one she'll wear for the short-est time—her wedding gown—will probably say more about her and her dreams than any other piece of clothing she'll ever own.

A wedding gown is a ticket to a woman's ideal image of herself at the happiest time in her life, a time that will be documented and remembered by family and friends for years to come in framed photographs.

It is likely to be the most expensive item of clothing you'll ever purchase—unless you borrow a dress, wear an heirloom, or find other creative ways to save money on your gown. And you'll wear it for all of about six hours, but those are six monumental hours.

There is no question that selecting your dress signals a big decision, which has to do with more than just how you look on that day. Your choice of wedding gown has a big

This classic evening wedding dress
is timeless—even your mother
would approve. And the clean
lines, fitted bodice, and flowing
skirt flatter most body types.

impact on almost every other aspect of your wedding as well. It helps to determine the level of formality and the tone of the entire affair. A more modern gown might indicate an urban setting with very clean, simple decor and flowers; a more romantic gown might mean more elaborate, ornate touches. Your choice of dress affects what everyone else in the wedding party will be wearing. Certain dresses are also more appropriate than others, depending on the timing of the wedding. A Saturday night wedding warrants a more formal gown than a Sunday afternoon affair, for example.

Obviously, your dress is an important factor in your wedding scheme, which should be determined early on in your planning. In fact, it can take between four and six months to get the dress you want, and to have it fitted, so you should tend to this early in the game.

In the first chapter of this book, I recommended writing a paragraph for yourself about your vision of the wedding. You might want to include in that paragraph what your dress is going to be like.

When you go shopping and scouting around, do your best to keep your vision in mind. It will be easy to be swayed by beautiful dresses that have nothing to do with what you've visualized. But you want to maintain a solid concept in your mind that carries over smoothly from one aspect of your wedding to another.

Where to Begin

Shopping for a wedding dress can be an emotional, exhausting experience. There are a few ways to approach it, and it helps to know what type of shopper you are—and to go with people who are very close to you, whose opinions you trust. Bring a close girlfriend, or your mother, or someone with whom you can have a good time—not someone who will get bored by the experience.

There are different types of bridal stores, and depending on your budget and your temperament, you'll be more comfortable in some places than others. For instance, in Brooklyn, New York, there's the world-famous bridal discounter, Kleinfeld's. The place is a virtual wedding gown emporium, with an encyclopedic selection. But there are always lots of people there, and the breadth of merchandise can be overwhelming. Some brides who want a more low-key experience and have a more honed vision of what they want their dress to look like prefer to go to Kleinfeld's boutique at Saks Fifth Avenue in Manhattan instead, where the selection is narrower and the atmosphere is more upscale.

There are certainly many other bridal shops, representing a broad spectrum of price ranges and styles, from small, local boutiques with lots of traditional dresses, to more cutting-edge bridal boutiques, such as the well-known Vera Wang shop on Madison Avenue in New York, which is filled with lots of sleek, elegant, updated designs.

Many department stores, of different calibers, have bridal departments. One bride I know, Sari, got her gown very inexpensively at J. C. Penney, on Long Island. Sari didn't have a big budget, so she decided to check out the selection at Penney's. Her gown was ivory-colored satin and lace with a straight sheath bottom and a peplum at the waist—it was 1989, the year of the peplum. It was a discontinued sample, which cost her only about $350.

But although it was a very attractive dress, in hindsight, Sari says it wasn't really very "her," and this brings up the issue of taking the time to make sure your dress is really right. Sari was hasty in choosing a wedding dress because she didn't have the patience at the time, and she didn't think she would like the experience of shopping in a variety of

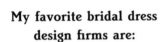

My favorite bridal dress design firms are:

Vera Wang, Morgan Le Fay, Ilissa, Galina, Bill Levkoff, and Signature Design.

See the Resources list on page 163 for information on how to locate these labels at stores near you.

THE BEAUTIFUL BRIDE

This sleek, elegant design—characterized by a minimum of lace, beads, and ruffles—is typical of some of the dresses found in the Vera Wang boutique in New York. Her dresses are also sold in some major department stores throughout the country. Refer to the Resource list on page 163 for information about availability.

bridal boutiques. Looking back, she says she wishes she had taken more time and chosen something less trendy, because she cringes when she looks at her wedding pictures.

But the point is, it was a good-quality, attractive dress, bought off the rack for a moderate amount of money. So there are inexpensive dresses out there.

Into the Dressing Room

Wherever you choose to shop for your wedding gown, whether it's in one store or many, bear in mind that you'll need an appointment. It can take three weeks to a month just to get an appointment, so take care of this as early on as you can. This is generally how bridal shops and departments work, across the board, because you really do need the undivided attention of a salesperson.

I find that a lot of women, when they go shopping for their wedding gown, bring along pictures from bridal magazines to show the saleswomen what they're interested in. When you get there, you might be deceived by the limited selection on display and think they might not have what you're looking for. But, in many shops, the majority of the dresses are stored in back.

The experience of shopping for a wedding gown is quite different from shopping for other types of clothes, because there's no such thing as self-service. You cannot just sift through racks, grab something in your size, and take it into the dressing room to try on. The whole time you are in a bridal shop you interact with a salesperson.

I think it's really important to have a good idea of what you're looking for before you go to the store—in terms of color, style, weight of the fabric, and any ornamentation you might want on the dress—but still keep an open mind. Often

Off-the-rack dresses that need a minimum of alterations are a great option for budget-minded brides. But make your selection carefully—you'll be seeing your dress in wedding pictures for *years* to come. This column of creamy, silky chiffon was bought off-the-rack in the evening gown department of Saks Fifth Avenue. Paired with a great headpiece, shoes, and flowers, it's a thoroughly modern look.

the salespeople will bring out dresses that don't look like they're your style and suggest you try them on. I recommend that you go with the flow, because you might discover that there are things which look good on you that you might not have considered on your own. These women are accustomed to dealing with lots of brides, and they know their selection of dresses very well.

It's important to be open and forthcoming with the salesperson assigned to you. Brides often ask me, "How can they have me try on dresses when they don't know my personality?" The answer is that you should allow enough time to talk frankly with the salesperson and let her get to know you and your taste a bit. However, if you find that you don't get along with the salesperson who has been assigned to you, you should let the store management know and ask to have someone else appointed. This is a very important—and expensive—decision and it's essential that you feel comfortable and well tended to.

Other things to bear in mind about shopping for dresses:

- You might want to bring a bottle of water to drink, because the fabric from all the dresses absorbs most of the moisture in the air, and you can easily become dehydrated.
- Wear clothes that are easy to get in and out of, so that you can go in and out of the dressing room quickly if you want to scan the racks again between try-ons.
- Remember that the dresses you try on might be a little discolored and threadbare because they've been tried on so many times by so many brides before you. Don't let the conditions of the dresses be off-putting.
- Once you choose your gown, don't forget to ask for a swatch of the fabric so that you can get your shoes dyed to match.

- If you have a strapless bra, bring it with you so that you can get an accurate idea of what off-the-shoulder styles will look like on you.
- Don't expect the gown you try on to fit you perfectly. It will be tailored to your body over the course of several fittings.

A Lexicon of Basic Wedding Dress Terms

When trying on wedding dresses at bridal shops, you'll find yourself faced with a whole new vocabulary that describes the different components of a dress. Familiarize yourself with these terms and you'll be way ahead of the game. You'll know how to ask for what you like—and tell your salesperson just exactly what you want to avoid.

DRESSES

Ball gown: The most traditional wedding dress style. Involves a full skirt, tapered waist, and fitted bodice. Often the ball gown style requires a *Crinoline*, a stiff skirt made of tulle worn under the skirt that creates a dramatic pouff and lots of volume. Scarlett O'Hara was partial to crinolines.

Empire: A dress style first popularized in nineteenth-century France. Characterized by a fitted bodice that gathers right below the bustline and flares out to a graceful skirt. Think Gwyneth Paltrow's ingenue fashions in *Emma.*

Sheath: A modern, sexier take on the wedding dress theme. This is usually a long column of silky fabric, nipped at the waist. Variations of the sheath style can include a *Trumpet hemline*, which means that the sheath flares out slightly at the knee to create a conical "trumpet" shape. This look requires the wearer to take baby steps (think Morticia in *The Addams Family*), but it's a very flattering silhouette.

NECKLINES

High: A Victorian-inspired neckline that fits close to the neck and is often embellished with pearls and lace.

Jewel: The simplest neckline of them all. In everyday parlance, a jewel neckline is a round, crewneck-style neckline that circles the base of the throat.

Sabrina: Very 1950s. Very elegant. This neckline follows the contour of the collarbone, from shoulder to shoulder. Think Audrey Hepburn in (you guessed it) *Sabrina.*

Sweatheart: An old-fashioned term for a sculpted neckline shaped like the top half of a heart.

SLEEVES

Cap: Short, fitted sleeves, usually paired with a fitted bodice. This sleeve/bodice combination is a flattering look for most body types.

Dolman: Big, exaggerated, billowing sleeves that puff out from the armhole and gather at the wrist.

Leg-of-mutton: Not unlike the Dolman style, this sleeve puffs out from the armhole in a less exaggerated way and tapers snugly at the wrist. This style of sleeve is often a component of a high-collared Victorian-style dress.

Three-quarter: Fitted sleeves that end just below the elbow. A classic, ladylike look.

FABRICS

You'll find that wedding dresses are made of a combination of fabrics of varying weights and textures. For example, a silk charmeuse sheath style dress can feature a sweetheart neckline constructed entirely of body-revealing "Illusion" (see definition below). Following are some commonly used dress materials:

Brocade: A weighty, rich silk fabric with raised patterns. Creates a formal, dramatic, Renaissance look.

Charmeuse: A lustrous, silky fabric that drapes beautifully.

Chiffon: A flowing, sheer silk or rayon fabric that's lightweight and extremely feminine.

Illusion: A new kind of stretchy, body-conscious, completely sheer fabric first popularized by wedding dress designer Vera Wang. Used to create dramatic, sexy necklines.

Moiré: A heavy, silk taffeta with subtle, wavy water designs.

Organza: A sheer, stiff fabric that's similar to tulle but is made of a more closely woven material.

Shantung: A silky fabric with an irregular, nubby surface.

Taffeta: A crisp, lustrous, silky fabric that gives definition to bodices and adds lots of volume to full skirts.

Tulle: A sheer, stiff fabric most associated with wedding day garments. Usually made of silk, rayon, or nylon, this material is used for veils and crinolines.

A Pop Quiz for Brides-to-Be

A visit to a bridal shop can be an overwhelming and stressful experience. The array of choices and possibilities is dizzying. But if you have a strong sense of how you'd like to look on your wedding day, you can conquer your anxiety and cut straight to the chase with your salesperson.

Take this quiz *before* you start cruising the stores for dress ideas. Of course, your vision of yourself as a bride may evolve slightly as you actually try on dresses. However, this run-through should at least acquaint you with some of the questions you'll encounter when you venture into the realm of the wedding dress emporium . . .

What is your price range? $_____ to $_____

When is your wedding taking place? Month _____, Day_____, Year_____

What time of the day will your wedding be held?

Would you characterize your wedding as a formal or informal event?

Will the men be required to wear black tie or dark suits or will they be dressed more casually? (Your answer to this question will help you determine the degree of formality of your dress.)

Will your wedding be held outdoors or indoors?

Your bridal style can be best characterized by the following phrase(s):

a. I am a romantic, traditional bride who favors flounces and ruffles.
b. I am a sleek, modern bride who favors strong, sexier silhouettes.
c. I never pictured myself wearing a traditional wedding dress.
d. I don't have a strong feeling about wedding dresses—I'd like to see a variety of different styles and choose the one that looks best.

Are there any aspects of your body that you want to accentuate or deaccentuate?

Circle the decorative elements that you'd like to incorporate into your wedding dress:

lace

beads

sequins

rhinestones

pearls

flounces and ruffles

silk flowers (rosettes)

None of the above—I prefer clean lines and minimal detail.

Do you prefer stiff, more formal fabrics (like taffeta) or more relaxed materials, such as chiffon and charmeuse silk?

What kind of silhouette do you prefer? (check one):

Flouncy ball gown with or without a crinoline?

A fitted bodice?

Straight sheath that is tailored to the body but appears more demure than sexy?

A body-conscious gown that shows off curves?

A smart, modern suit?

What length dress do you prefer? (check one):

A hemline that grazes the tops of the feet?

A tea-length sheath that grazes the tops of the ankles?

A short, knee-length (or shorter) dress?

Do you plan to wear flats or high heels?

Do you plan to wear a veil?

Do you plan to wear a train?

Briefly describe dress styles you've seen in bridal magazines that you definitely like . . .

Briefly describe dress styles you've seen in bridal magazines that you definitely dislike . . .

Dressing on the Side

You're in the dressing room, you're trying on a number of dresses, and there's one you like—except for the sleeves, or the shade of cream or white, or some other detail. This doesn't necessarily mean that you haven't found your wedding gown.

One of the biggest misconceptions about bridal gowns is that they come only as seen in the bridal magazines or in the stores. In fact, most gowns are offered in a variety of versions, so it pays to ask very specific questions, such as what other materials and shades the gown comes in, or whether it can be ordered with shorter sleeves, or without the sleeves altogether. Sometimes, if a bride is shopping for a gown during a season that has the opposite weather from the season she'll be getting married in, the dresses will be shown in a different weight than would be appropriate. A dress you see in January could be displayed in a heavy-weight material with long sleeves—but it might be available in a lighter fabric, and sleeveless. The key is to ask.

Most dresses can be ordered in alternative forms or can be custom-made for you. If you say to yourself, "I love this dress, I love the color, I love the way the bodice is fitting, but I don't like the sleeves and the bows," it's very easy to say "Take the bows off and put capped sleeves on it."

Of course, the more you stray from the basic dress, the more it will cost you. Each alteration costs money, so keep that in mind. If you find a dress that requires major adjusting in terms of style, ask whether that same designer has other styles you can try on. Chances are, your dream dress already exists. Also, bear in mind that you will probably never see the version of the dress that you have formulated until very close to the wedding.

A ball gown—style dress that was once designed with an off-the-shoulder bodice with no rosettes. This bride had her dress altered to meet her specifications with a minimum of fuss and an eye on her budget.

There are lots of little alterations that can be made to your dress by adding or subtracting padding in different areas. If you're looking for a fuller bustline, talk to the salesperson about having breast padding sewn in. If your dress comes with shoulder pads, you might want to remove them for a softer look. Don't be shy about exploring all the options of each dress.

The Perfect Gown for You

Every bride has a different vision of herself and the kind of dress she wants to wear on her wedding day. Choosing a dress is very much a matter of personal taste. These days, there are so many options beyond the standard and traditional—and that's refreshing.

My eye tends to gravitate toward very simple, classic, but updated designs with very little embellishment. To achieve a clean, elegant look, I think it's important not to choose too many elements on your gown. You don't want to have pearls *and* rhinestones *and* sequins. I've seen a lot of dresses with simple lace cutouts, or embroidery, or tone-on-tone texture, or simple flower rosettes, and so many of them are really beautiful.

But taste is not the only factor to consider in choosing a dress. There are other elements that come into play, such as body type.

Your body type and your weight are important to keep in mind. One of the first things women do when they get engaged is go on a diet so that they'll be at an ideal weight for the big day. But *do not* put too much pressure on yourself by buying a dress that's a smaller size than you usually wear. It's a lot easier to take in a larger dress than it is to let out

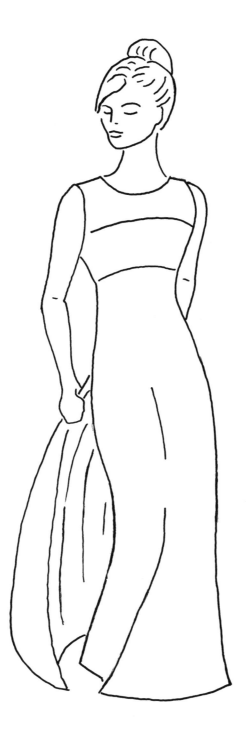

For the petite bride: not too much volume or ornamentation for a small, trim figure.

For the larger bride: a classical, elegant shape updated with the simplest of lines. Look for a full skirt and narrowing waist for a truly flattering silhouette.

a smaller dress. Over the course of a few months, you will go for a number of fittings, and if you are able to lose the weight, then the dress can be altered accordingly.

If you're conscious about a part of your body, like your arms or your bust, take this into consideration as you shop. Don't think that because you're having a summer wedding you have to wear a sleeveless or off-the-shoulder dress. You can choose a dress that covers your arms if that makes you more comfortable. It beats squirming in front of the camera to try to hide them.

If you have very full hips and you want to play them down, don't feel as if you have to wear the crinoline in your gown. The crinoline is optional. Some women just find that a crinoline makes a wedding gown too costumey and don't want it. You'd be surprised at how flattering some of those pouffier gowns can be without the crinoline underneath.

Also consider whether you're someone who would be comfortable wearing a full-length gown. It can be appropriate to wear a shorter gown, even for a Saturday night affair. I've seen lots of beautiful dresses that come to just below the knee, which are just as dressy and sophisticated as full-length gowns. Really, it's a matter of personal taste and what you're comfortable with. But if you're going to wear a shorter dress, you really shouldn't wear plain, dyed-to-match shoes. Your shoes will matter more with a shorter dress, so make them count.

It's also a good idea to keep in mind how animated you are as you try on dresses. While you are in the privacy of your dressing room, you might want to try to lift your arms up and even dance a little—as silly as that might seem—to make sure that the dress you're trying on won't fall off or shift too much when you're celebrating.

One bride I know, Amy, regrets not doing this. She wore an incredible dress, like the one in the Estée Lauder Beautiful ad. It was very off-the-shoulder, but she is a very full-busted

A short dress with a hemline that just grazes the knee shows off your great legs. Just be sure to accessorize with a special pair of shoes.

woman. And every time she lifted her arms up, her bust threatened to spill out of the dress.

So make sure you move around in the dresses you're trying on.

Dressing to Flatter . . .

We all have fixed ideas about aspects of our bodies we'd like to accentuate and the features we'd just as soon disguise. The following are some general guidelines for helping you choose a dress that will complement your figure and make you feel 100 percent comfortable—all wedding day–long.

Petite

- The watchword for petite women is *elongate*.
- Avoid dress styles that involve voluminous amounts of fabric.
- The combination of a fitted bodice and full skirt will make a small woman look squat and truncated.
- Stick to more tailored, body-conscious shapes and open, sexier necklines (sweetheart and off-the-shoulder styles work beautifully).
- Skip the long veil and opt for a shorter waist-skimming or shoulder-skimming alternative.
- Look for a sheath or Empire-style dress—these shapes create a long, uninterrupted line.

Tall

- Tall women look great in a wide variety of styles—the trick is determining what you want.
- The sheath-style dress is an option, but it's not a good bet if you are extremely flat chested.

- Don't opt for a Victorian-style dress with long sleeves and a high collar.
- Accentuate your collarbone with a fitted bodice and open neckline.
- Look for a fuller skirt made of a rich, sumptuous fabric.
- Long veils work well on a tall figure; just be careful not to pair the long veil with a high up-'do—too much height is not a good thing.

Heavy Hips

- Heavier women need to create a sculpted, trim silhouette—look for dresses made of taffeta and other stiff fabrics to help you achieve a trim, tailored shape.
- Your undergarments are very important—purchase a corset or girdle that flattens the stomach and emphasizes the waist.
- Don't wear shoulder pads (it's a misconception that oversized shoulders balance wide hips), but emphasize the line of the shoulders by selecting a dress with an Illusion top. You'll create the feeling of bareness while still achieving some coverage.
- Skip the tight bodice and instead opt for a top with a soft, rounded edge finished with inward-facing box pleats.

Long Torso and Short Legs

- Your mission is to create a long, uninterrupted line—don't choose a dress that has a well-defined bodice, waist, and skirt.
- A sheath style is a flattering option—consider a straight sheath with a cutout back.
- Select a dress that reaches the ankle—stay away from calf-length and short dresses.

Heavy Arms

- You're not alone if you feel self-conscious about your arms—lots of women want to cover up their arms, particularly their upper arms.
- Achieve coverage, but still allow for some sexy bareness by selecting a dress with a sweetheart neckline lined in Illusion fabric.
- Choose a dramatic long sleeve that extends through the middle of the hand or a three-quarter-length sleeve that covers the upper arms.

Voluptuous and Busty

- Voluptuous women have two choices—either to accentuate their beautiful curves or to minimize their shape.
- To accentuate a full bust, choose a foundation garment (shorthand for a supportive bra) that's uplifting and wear an off-the-shoulder, open bodice. Just be careful not to overdo the bareness. And, of course, move around in your dress during fittings to make sure you're not spilling out of it.
- To deaccentuate curves, wear a one-piece minimizing undergarment—a bodysuit—under a fitted bodice with a jewel neck and cap sleeves. Balance with a full skirt. The idea is to emphasize your waist, not your bust.

Flat Chested

- Take the emphasis off the chest and instead highlight the graceful line of the collarbone with an open, off-the-shoulder neckline.

- Choose a dress style with a dramatic, cutout back and cinched waist.
- Balance out the overall silhouette with a flowing skirt that drapes your figure in a flattering way.
- Opt for a realistic-looking padded bra or have a dressmaker actually sew a bustline into your dress to create shape.
- Stay away from darted bodices made of stiff fabrics like taffeta. Even if a bustline is sewn into this type of bodice, the end result could be somewhat artificial looking.

Broad Shoulders

- Broad shoulders are fabulous-looking—expose them!
- When broad shoulders are covered up, the effect is boxy and unattractive.
- Select a dress with a narrow bodice that offsets your shoulders and creates an hourglass shape.
- Consider wearing an off-the-shoulder neckline and long sleeves—you'll look supremely elegant.

All Dressed in White

Your skin color is important to keep in mind as you shop for a wedding gown. You'll look radiant in a dress that's a flattering hue for your skin tone—and you'll look sallow in the wrong color.

White is the color we all associate with wedding gowns. But white-white is a very difficult color for many people to wear, even in regular, everyday clothing. Fortunately, there are many different shades of white when it comes to wedding gowns.

Colors range from stark white all the way to a café-au-lait, antique sort of tone. There are whites that have a very slight pastel tint to them, in pinks, greens, blues, and other hues.

Whatever your coloring is, I recommend *not* getting a tan for your wedding. The contrast between tan skin and any shade of white is much too great. So, when you're shopping for your dress, imagine that your skin tone won't be too far from what is normal for you. It's a good idea to bring a pinky/peachy lipstick that you like along with you, so that it will help you visualize your wedding-day coloring more accurately.

Use your judgment in choosing a color of wedding gown. If you're olive skinned, wearing a very white dress would probably not be such a great choice. If you're very fair, with light or red hair, a white-white dress or a pastel-tinted gown is a strong option. If you're African-American, with darker skin, you might want to veer toward deeper tones of ivory and cream to complement your complexion. In any case, the idea is to have your dress complement, not contrast, with your skin.

The Train

For many women, the idea of a wedding gown is accompanied by the image of a long train extending from the back of the dress. But trains are not for everyone, and all trains are not created equal.

Trains can go from a few feet long to many yards and often add a majestic touch to the bride's appearance. They can also be terribly cumbersome and difficult to get used to.

There are usually options in terms of train lengths. Most trains can be bustled up with buttons for the reception. But it's also possible to find dresses with removable trains that attach with Velcro just for the wedding ceremony.

Selecting the right shade of white . . .

White is a tricky color. The wrong shade of white can make an otherwise rosy complexion look flat and sallow. Here are a few easy guidelines that will help you find the shade of white that coordinates perfectly with your skin tone.

For cool and fair skin tones—choose a light champagne white or icy white.

For fair skin with warm undertones—choose a sheer organza in ivory, not quite white.

For skin with yellow or olive undertones—choose a vanilla satin white.

For freckly redheads—choose a creamy satin white.

For women of color or dark skin—choose a true white-white for great contrast.

Wedding gowns tend to close with lots of tiny buttons in the back. Make no mistake: It is a hassle to fasten them all, so appoint someone from your wedding party to do this for you—someone you can count on to be patient and have calm hands on that day.

Sometimes vintage and heirloom dresses will have perspiration stains or some yellowing—or armpit odor. These trouble spots can be taken care of, either through dry cleaning or by removing the fabric under the arm and replacing it with new fabric (this is something a dressmaker can do for you).

A train isn't an absolutely necessary component of the dress. In fact, lots of the newer, more modern sheath dresses tend not to have trains on them. Some women will opt instead for a beautiful mantilla, or long piece of lace, as their headpiece, which extends like a train, to the floor. Another option is to wear a three-tiered veil, with the longest piece of it being six to eight feet in length and acting as a train.

The Ultimate Hand-Me-Down

Wearing a dress that's been handed down from a mother, grandmother, or close friend can be a really special touch, and it can be economical as well, even if major alterations are required. Wearing an heirloom dress can be much more meaningful than purchasing a completely new one.

If you don't have a hand-me-down dress to wear, another option is to purchase a vintage dress. They're quite a bit less expensive than new gowns and provide an old-world, nostalgic flavor. And there's something romantic about wearing a dress that someone else wore down the aisle before you. There are more and more antique bridal shops in many cities around the country.

But you shouldn't feel pressured to wear a dress that's been in the family if the style doesn't fit your taste or personality. Dresses from some decades have a more timeless feeling than those from other times. Gowns from the fifties and sixties don't have quite the lasting appeal of dresses from the forties and before.

You don't have to wear an heirloom or vintage dress in its entirety. The nice thing about these dresses is that they come apart pretty easily, and can be altered. And parts of them can be combined with new elements.

For instance, one of the brides I worked with, Jill,

wanted to wear her mother's dress, but she was a lot smaller than her mother. Jill found a way to rework the dress so that it looked right on her. She had a seamstress take the top off her mother's dress and turn it around so that the V that was in the back at the waist was now in the front. She also had the train removed and the skirt narrowed to fit her.

With a good tailor or seamstress you trust and a bit of imagination, it's very easy to rework an old dress. You can take sleeves off, you can put an old top on a new skirt—and make it your own.

The Alternative Bride

I'm finding that more and more women are choosing an alternative look for their wedding. I'm in favor of coordinating your own personal fashion style into your wedding and choosing to wear an evening dress, a cocktail dress, or a suit. And this is not just for second or subsequent weddings. John Kennedy, Jr.'s bride, Carolyn Bessette, wore a very simple gown that was almost not bridal-looking, and she was the picture of elegance and refinement.

One client of mine, Noreen, wore a gown by the designer Morgan Le Fay that was not originally conceived as a wedding gown. A producer of television commercials, her style is crisp, modern, and sophisticated. But she accessorized her flowing, vanilla-colored dress with satin shoes and simple pearl-and-diamond jewelry. And she became a bridal vision.

Another bride I know of, Ricki, got married in a long, off-white sheath dress which she bought in an evening dress department of a department store. It was a copy of an Armani gown. She wore a chiffony shawl around her shoulders and flowers in her hair. She looked amazing.

So, it is possible to imprint your own personal bridal style onto a gown that was intended for something else.

This bride wears a two-tier
detachable train that attaches with
Velcro to her headpiece. Once the
ceremony concludes, she can
remove the train. Elbow-length
gloves complete the picture.

When Carolyn Bessette married John F. Kennedy, Jr., in this sheath dress, the fashion community applauded. She chose an evening gown rather than a traditional wedding dress—and the result was spectacular.

The ten biggest style mistakes brides make:

1. Not moving around when you try on your dress. In the privacy of your fitting room (be sure to close the curtain!), put your arms over your head, sit down, practice dancing. You'll be glad you put your gown to the test.

2. Wearing shoulder pads in your dress. Shoulder pads can make you look dated.

3. Not learning how to button or drape your dress properly before the wedding day. If you can't do this, find someone in your wedding party who can.

4. Not setting aside the correct undergarments for your wedding day. Purchase all special undergarments (backless bra, seamless panties, 2 pairs of panty hose, etc.) after you've bought your dress.

continued

Foundation Garments—the Real Story

A chapter on wedding dresses would not be complete without an investigative report on the wonders of foundation garments—underwear, that is. And as a knowledgeable lingerie saleswoman once told me, "If you thought finding a good man was hard, just try to find the right underwear to wear with your bridal gown." Actually, with a little information and some patience, you'll find just the right undergarments for your wedding ensemble.

Your undergarments can be purchased at any major department store that has a pretty extensive selection of lingerie. You should have the appropriate undergarments purchased by the time you head off to your first wedding dress fitting—don't leave this important task for the last minute!

When you embark on this project, keep in mind one key word: *seamlessness*. You'll always look sleek and pulled together so long as your panties and bra are not creating a distinct outline underneath your dress. Look for seamless panties made by Maidenform, Bali, and On Gossamer. The best seamless bras are made by Maidenform, On Gossamer, Parisa, and Natori.

Strapless or backless bras are often good options for brides wearing scooped or off-the-shoulder necklines. Natori, Carnival, and Va Bien's Absolute Backless Bra are excellent choices. Old-fashioned stays, boning, and waist closures ensure that these bras are supportive—and invisible under your low-cut gown.

Padded bras are enduringly popular choices for brides. Natori, On Gossamer, and Maidenform are the labels I'd recommend. If you're a Wonderbra devotee, just keep in mind that wearing these miraculous garments can be uncomfortable over a long period of time. They create great cleavage, but make sure you can stand the pain.

An effective way to achieve a fuller bustline is to place silicone inserts (available at most department stores) in your bra. No, this procedure does not involve any surgery. These little wonders are fairly expensive—$150—but they create a very natural look.

Of course, the best option of all is having your seamstress sew your bra into your dress. Bring your bra to your first dress fitting and inquire about having this done.

The right bra can make a huge difference in the way your figure looks beneath your gown. But if you are interested in truly reshaping and resculpting your body (and minimizing certain figure flaws), consider buying what is now being called shapewear. In your grandmother's day, this kind of item was referred to as a girdle or corset. New high-tech fabrics and designs, however, have made these figure-enhancing garments fairly comfortable. Look for the labels Va Bien, Lily of France, and Flexees. Each of these manufacturers makes support panties, waist cinchers, and extremely supportive bras. Va Bien, in particular, carries a unitard in an uplifting and minimizing Lycra-and-polyester blend. For a seamless, slim look, this one-piece foundation garment is the way to go.

Naturally, every bride wants to wear sexy, feminine, frilly lingerie under her wedding dress. Garters and stockings seem like an appropriate combo for the occasion, but they can look quite bulky, especially under a sheer or revealing gown. And there's always the risk that one of the stays may pop open, creating a potentially embarrassing situation (a stocking that has fallen down around your ankle). My advice: Skip the fancy stuff and opt instead for lingerie that's attractive but functional.

5. **Being cold and having nothing available to wear as a wrap or jacket.** Try not to resort to throwing an old ski parka over your lovely wedding gown. . . . Purchase or, better yet, borrow an appropriate shawl, wrap, or dress coat for the occasion.

6. **Putting on your lipstick before you put on your dress**—and getting it on your dress. I've seen this happen countless times. Don't make this mistake!

7. **Overaccessorizing.**

8. **Too much crinoline for too small a woman.**

9. **Not practicing walking in your gown, shoes, and headpiece.** If you move awkwardly in your gown, you'll spoil the effect. Practice makes perfect.

10. **Not making sure your groom is as organized as you are.** If he doesn't look good, you don't look good. Enough said.

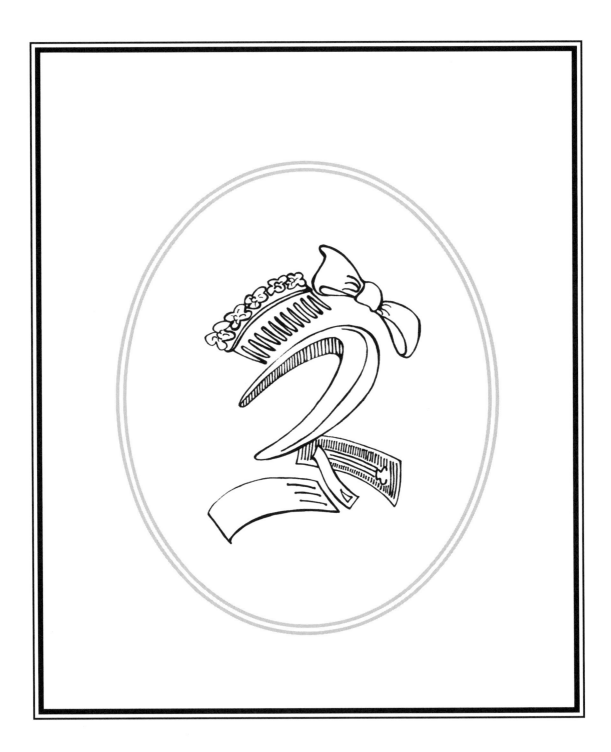

Your Veil and Headpiece . . . Accessorizing with a Flourish

3

I T'S NOT EVERY DAY OF A WOMAN'S LIFE THAT SHE wears a crownlike ornament and a veil—at least not in American culture. The headpiece and veil are accessories that are unique to the wedding day. These accessories are probably unfamiliar to you—that's why you need to consider them carefully from the outset, when you determine the overall look you want to achieve.

Not everyone has a firm understanding of veils and headpieces, and it's understandable since this is very unusual headgear, worn maybe once in a lifetime. The headpiece and veil are usually two separate objects. The headpiece is a decorative hair accessory that traditionally remains stationary throughout the day of the wedding; the veil is a detachable screen of lace or tulle that is put in place usually just for the ceremony. Headpieces often incorporate combs, barrettes, and headbands, but these things are not meant to hold up your hair. Your hairdo must stand on its own, and the rest of the accessories are decoration.

Bear in mind that not every bride feels comfortable wearing a headpiece and veil, or feels it's necessary. In these modern times, some brides depart from the time-worn tradition of wearing a veil, even if they decide to wear a headpiece. I personally don't think either is absolutely necessary. If you decide to forgo either a headpiece or veil or both, consider your hairdo a more important aspect of your wedding ensemble. It's not that your hairdo should be more ornate, but it should certainly look more special than it does on an average day at the office. Without a headpiece, you can consider wearing just a special hair ornament or a longer pair of earrings.

If you plan to wear a headpiece and/or a veil, you should certainly think about what you want your headpiece and veil to look like when you shop for your dress. You need to figure these accessories—and the way you plan to wear your hair—into your overall vision. Keep in mind your proportions; if you're a petite woman, and you're choosing a full dress, a big headpiece and a long veil won't work. You'll get lost in them.

Once you've chosen a dress, you can begin looking for a headpiece. I recommend trying on as many as you can, because there are numerous options, and you want to find something that is going to complete your wedding ensemble in a simple, complementary way. There really is a wide range of types of headpieces: you can opt for one worn quite close to the front of your forehead, to those that sit nicely behind the crown of your head. When selecting a headpiece, the issues to consider are: style, color, proportion, and fit.

Most bridal shops carry headpieces and veils, so you can usually try them on right there in the store as you are trying on dresses. You might get lucky and find your headpiece and

This bride has chosen to forgo the traditional veil and wears her hair in a dramatic topknot cinched with a piece of satin.

dress at the same time, making it much easier to coordinate all the elements of your wedding ensemble.

There are also specialty shops that custom design headpieces and veils. Sometimes the easiest alternative is to have these important accessories made to your specifications. (If you're looking in the yellow pages, these specialty shops are probably listed as milliners or hat stores.) Again, ask questions and try on as many samples as possible until you find a headpiece and veil that fit your vision perfectly. Bring photographs of your dress and swatches of the material so that you'll be able to match the color and texture exactly. If you haven't got an exact picture in your head of what you want your headpiece to look like, it's a good idea to clip some pictures from bridal magazines that show headpieces that are along the lines of what you're thinking of.

The Icing on the Cake

It's important that your headpiece and veil work with everything else—your dress, your hair, your other accessories—rather than stand out considerably. This means you'll be very limited as to the type of hairdo you can have. You don't want to look overdone, or costumey, or not like yourself. If you are going to wear a veil with your headpiece and you have hair that's chin length or longer, it's a good idea to wear the front part of your hair back or up. You probably don't want to wear your hair completely down if you're going to be wearing a veil. Usually, when brides tell me they want to wear their hair down for their wedding, I try to get them to agree to a style that is half down, half up.

One really nice way of doing this is to take the front of the hair, pull it up into a ponytail for a little bit of height, then take a strip of the hair from below and wrap it

Here's a simple headpiece-and-veil combination: a barrette covered with silk anchoring a waist-length swatch of tulle (which is sewn onto the inside of the barrette). Note the half-down, half-up hairdo.

around the holder, and hold it in place with two bobby pins, so it looks like a knot of hair. This way, when you take your veil off, you still have a sleek, nice hairdo. And you can wear almost any kind of headpiece with it.

However you choose to wear your hair on your wedding day, I recommend trying on headpieces with your hair at least casually styled the way you want it to look for the big day, even if you just put it up loosely in a twist. This is really the only method of assessing whether the look will work for you.

My least favorite style of headpiece is a tiara. Their glitter and formality distract the eye away from the overall picture. Also, because most tiaras are held in place with two combs, they are not easy to get out of your hair without messing it up.

Most brides only remove the veil after the ceremony and leave the headpiece on during the reception. Sometimes, though, the headpiece is uncomfortable, and you might want to remove it. So make sure you either have a headpiece that is easily removable or that you or someone in your bridal party knows how to take it out gracefully.

Because a headpiece and veil are things you're not accustomed to wearing, it's also a good idea to practice wearing them, the same way that you should practice wearing your wedding shoes a couple of times before the big day.

> While you're practicing walking around wearing your headpiece, also get used to the idea that just after your ceremony, lots of people are going to be hugging you—and pulling at your veil in the process, possibly messing up your hair. If you're planning to wear a long veil, perhaps practice taking it around the side of your neck and draping it over your arm.

A tiara sets a formal, dramatic tone that seems out of sync with the trend toward more understated weddings.

A Lexicon of Basic Veil Terms

Many of the options mentioned in this chapter are modern, creative reinterpretations of traditional styles of veils. But when you shop for veils, be prepared to decode some of the traditional veil terminology you'll encounter along the way. Here's a quick summary of terms relating to veils:

Blusher: A very ladylike veil worn over the face. After the ceremony, the blusher is turned back over the headpiece.

Cathedral length: An even longer veil that extends roughly 3½ yards from the headpiece.

Chapel length: A dramatically long and formal veil that extends roughly 2½ yards from the headpiece.

Fingertip: A multilayered veil that reaches the fingertips.

Flyaway: An informal veil that usually consists of several layers of tulle that graze the shoulders.

Getting Creative

One of my favorite things is when people incorporate heirlooms into their headpieces or veils, whether they use a piece of lace from a mother's or grandmother's gown, or take flowers from an old gown and affix them with a simple hot glue gun to a comb that will hold the veil.

Making your own headpiece and veil, whether you use heirlooms or not, is certainly a viable option. Of course, this is a job for someone who likes craft projects. If you don't, leave it to the professionals. If you do, then trimming stores, sewing shops, fabric stores, and florists are your resources.

A mantilla-style veil is my all-time favorite look. It consists of a piece of lace or tulle attached to a comb or barrette. As this bride demonstrates, the mantilla works beautifully with upswept hair.

This bride wears a headband veil. The headband is slightly quilted for proportion and can be custom-decorated. A puffy tulle veil is attached with Velcro to the inside of the headband. When the veil is detached, the headband holds her hair in place all day.

A classic, no-frills veil: Attach a satin bow (glued to a barrette or comb) to a length of tulle with Velcro. Again, the tulle can be removed after the ceremony. This style is as easy to make as it is to wear.

To make your own headpiece, first you need to find the base—usually either a comb, a barrette, or a headband, made of plastic or covered with white material. If it's not already covered with white material, you can do that yourself, by getting a piece of the fabric from your dress or having a piece of fabric dyed to match and then covering the hair ornament with it, using a hot glue gun. You would wrap the hair ornament like a gift, making sure all the seams were tucked neatly underneath. You want the fabric to lie flat, so that it's not bulky on top of your head.

To decorate your headpiece, shop around for ornaments such as lace, small pearls, or fabric rosettes—but make sure you don't try to put too much ornamentation on your headpiece. Remember, as with so many other elements of your wedding ensemble, *less is more.*

Once you've chosen the embellishments, before fastening them permanently, try affixing them temporarily with straight pins, so that you're certain about how you want your headpiece decorated before you get stuck.

If you want to wear a veil, you can attach it to your headpiece with Velcro. Make sure you leave room on the underside of your headpiece to glue on one side of the Velcro. Also, you might want to have a veil in back, and a blusher veil in front. In this case, you'll need to leave room for two pieces of Velcro.

A veil can be as simple as a piece of tulle attached to a comb. To complete the look, have the tulle hemmed with a thin silk cord. For a more elaborate veil, instead of tulle, attach a piece of antique lace from a sideboard or tablecloth to a comb or barrette. Ask your dressmaker to pull this together for you—or if you're feeling creative (and are confident working with a needle and thread), do it yourself.

THE BEAUTIFUL BRIDE

Flower Girl

Fresh flowers are another very viable option for decorating your headpiece—or your hair—on your wedding day. You can either have your florist decorate your headpiece with flowers, or you can do it yourself. I don't really recommend doing it yourself, if you can avoid it, because it requires getting fresh flowers and doing arts and crafts with them either the day before or the day of your wedding so they'll be fresh—something you probably don't want to have to bother with at that time. So, if you can, I would recommend leaving this to the professionals.

But if you decide to decorate your own headpiece with flowers, you'll need to get to your florist prior to your wedding day and order some small flowers. You're looking for a stemmed flower with small, multiple buds on it, almost like a flower on a vine. Keep in mind when you're choosing these flowers that they should coordinate with the other flowers you've chosen to carry. They don't have to match exactly, but they should meld with the overall look.

Just as you might have done if you decorated your headpiece with pearls, lace, or fabric rosettes, first you'll want to cover your barrette, headband, or comb with fabric—this is done by wrapping the barrette, headband, or comb with fabric and adhering the fabric with a hot glue gun. Then, affix some Velcro to the underside of the headpiece where you want the veil or veils to be attached.

Next, you'll slowly arrange the flowers around your headpiece, first with straight pins, and finally attach them with hot craft glue. Give the flowers a little height, because your hair will likely cover up part of the headpiece. You can twist the vines, or stems, of the flowers around themselves so that they're thicker and more visible. You can also add some pearls—but go easy. And remember that a little glue goes a long way.

You might also forgo the headpiece and simply place flowers in your hair. You need to figure out what kinds of flowers you'd like to wear and where you want them to go. There are two people who should be involved in these decisions—your florist and the person doing your hair.

Go to your local florist and ask him to help you find some small flowers that will last through the day, and you might consider options other than baby's breath, which are my least favorite. And if you select fresh flowers, make sure they're subtle—like everything else that you choose for your wedding day.

Fresh flowers are usually worn in the hair in one of two ways—either placed along the pleat of a French twist or up-'do, or carefully woven into the hair at the crown of your head, creating a halo effect. But I offer one word of caution to all brides who plan to wear flowers in their hair: Don't attempt this project yourself. A few weeks before your wedding, have your hairdresser do a trial run, then plan to have the same stylist do your hair for your wedding. You can also appoint a skilled friend or family member to the task—provided that they've practiced placing the flowers in your hair beforehand and you liked the results.

Other Accessories

On your wedding day, there can be a temptation to wear every special piece of jewelry you've ever owned, or to buy really eye-catching earrings and other pieces. But the fact that this is a special day in your life does not mean that you should be completely decked out—it means exactly the op-

The overaccessorized bride: Wearing an elaborate headpiece and veil along with too much flashy jewelry (necklace, bracelets, and teardrop earrings) is a major fashion faux-pas. Remember, less is always more.

This bride got the message and pared down her accessories to a bare minimum. The effect is so much more glamorous and sophisticated.

Just because you have short hair doesn't mean you have to forgo wearing a veil. This bride affixed her veil to the back of her head with a decorated comb and lots of carefully concealed bobby pins.

posite. As is the case with so many elements of your wedding, when it comes to jewelry and accessories, think simplicity.

Your wedding is an occasion on which you want to be as simple and elegant as possible, letting the natural you radiate and shine forth. As it is, your wedding dress will command quite a bit of attention. Also, keep in mind you'll probably be wearing a headpiece and veil—accessories that you don't usually wear, which also draws a lot of attention. If you're wearing a prominent headpiece and a fairly elaborate hairdo, a lot of jewelry will just clutter the overall effect.

That doesn't mean you shouldn't wear any jewelry at all. But wearing earrings, a necklace, and a bracelet might just be too much at once. Even if you're wearing a dress that's off the shoulder with a fairly low neckline, it's really not necessary to wear a necklace. If you are going to wear one, though, it should be something simple, small, and refined, like perhaps a diamond drop or a set of small pearls. Here's a nice opportunity to incorporate an heirloom into your wedding ensemble, whether it's a necklace, simple earrings, or a bracelet that belonged to someone in your family or a friend.

Whatever jewelry you choose to wear on your wedding day should be special in some way, whether it has sentimental value or was a special gift. It should not be the jewelry you wear every day. Take off those rings and bracelets and things that have become part of the uniform of your day-to-day life for this one occasion.

Shoes Redux . . . Putting Your Best Foot Forward

4

THERE IS SO MUCH EMPHASIS PLACED ON A BRIDE'S gown, headpiece, hair, makeup, and accessories that shoes sometimes seem to take a backseat in importance—but they absolutely should not.

As a bride, you want to look elegant and chic—and coordinated—from head to toe, and so you must give as much thought to your wedding shoes as you do to any of your other bridal accoutrements.

Some people say, "What's the difference—you never really see the bride's shoes." But that's not at all true. A bride is always picking up the front of her dress because she's not used to walking in such a long gown, and the photographer will often ask a bride to put a foot forward for a portrait. So, it really does make a difference to have beautiful bridal shoes.

In fact, I consider your wedding shoes to be as important as your accessories and jewelry. Rather than taking the easy

way out and buying inexpensive dyed-to-match pumps, you might want to think about considering your wedding shoes as a way to express your own personal style on your wedding day. Take your time to choose shoes that are comfortable, but maybe allow yourself to be a little more daring in this area, especially if the rest of your wedding ensemble is toned down and simple.

If you've chosen a subtle dress, you can make a bit of a statement with your shoes. But don't go overboard with overaccessorizing. Nothing you wear on your wedding day should be overstated, including your shoes. If your shoes are going to have ornaments of any sort—lace, pearls, sequins, or rhinestones—try to choose only one of those elements. You don't need to wear everything at once. Less is still more, even if you're going to get a bit creative with your shoes.

Your shoes are the only part of your wedding ensemble that you'll probably be able to wear again—you can always dye them to wear for dressy occasions. Therefore, it's okay to splurge a little on shoes, and make sure they're extra special.

One bride I know who wears a size eleven shoe had a very difficult time finding wedding shoes that were beautiful yet still fit her. She wore a very modern, simple scoop-necked gown in matte jersey and wanted her shoes to be somewhat elaborate. She was willing to spend a bit more for the right shoes. When she finally found a shoe that she loved, she looked all over for it in her size. She even called the manufacturer. Her search paid off. She finally found a pair of the pearlized shoes, with a sculptured chunky heel and inlays in the fabric, and she plans to dye them black so she can wear them again and again.

Stepping Out

When is the right time to shop for your wedding shoes? Unfortunately, the best time is about a year before your wedding, because that's when the shoes that are appropriate for the season you're getting married in are being shown. If you're getting married in June and you're shopping for shoes in January, chances are, the more summery options will be limited. Spring or summer would be better times to shop, if you think way ahead.

You'll have more to choose from and you can just put your shoes away until your wedding day.

Of course, you're not going to purchase wedding shoes before you've chosen a wedding gown. But once that's taken care of, your shoes are the next decision you are going to make. And you'll want to make sure you have your shoes in time for your fittings, so that your dress can be hemmed at a length that's exactly right.

Ideally, you would want to shop for shoes at the same time that you buy your dress. But most bridal shops only carry pretty basic shoes, if they carry any at all.

We all know how tough it is to buy shoes for certain clothes without having those clothes with you. You can't lug your dress around to shoe stores, so you must bring along on your mission a Polaroid of the dress and a swatch of the fabric.

If the Shoe Fits

One of the first things to consider when buying your shoes is height—yours, your groom's, and the optimal height of your heels.

If you're a tall woman, close in height or taller than your groom, high heels might not be such a great choice. Of course, there is nothing anywhere that says a man has to be taller than his bride. There is no real protocol regarding this. It's all about how you and he feel about your relative heights.

Regardless of your height, if you're someone who doesn't regularly wear high heels and has difficulty walking in them, you might want to find a beautiful low, or flat, slipper rather than a high-heeled shoe. It's not absolutely necessary to wear high heels on your wedding day.

Another option is to have two different pairs of shoes—a higher pair to wear walking down the aisle and a lower pair for dancing at the reception.

Some more whimsical brides take this a step further, wearing decorated Keds or Converse high-tops at the reception so that they can really dance. But this tends to be a little childish and to detract from the elegance.

Whatever height shoe you choose to wear on your wedding day, make sure you practice walking in them, around the house, and not just once. You'll want to break your shoes in and get used to the feel of them, without soiling them.

Once you've determined the height of your heels, you must consider the thickness of the heels, especially if you're having an outdoor wedding. Pointy heels sink so easily into the ground. Also, if you're having an outdoor wedding, you might want to have a separate pair of shoes to wear outside for photographs, so that you don't get mud or grass stains on the shoes you're going to wear down the aisle and at the reception.

Fancy Footwork

So many brides choose basic, inexpensive, dyed-to-match pumps because they don't know that they have other options. But they do.

Even if you are on a tight budget, I recommend going to a department store and checking out the bridal shoes from some of the high-end designers and companies like Peter Fox, Manolo Blahnik, and Stuart Weitzman, just to get ideas. You may wind up ultimately buying your shoes from a less expensive source, like Nine West or Kenneth Cole, but you'll get some interesting ideas from the pricier lines.

Another option is being creative with inexpensive dyed-to-match shoes. With some lace, or pearls, or rhinestones—but please, just one of these options—and a hot glue gun, you can add some subtle, personal flair to an old standard.

Although many brides wear pumps, you're not limited to that style of shoe. During warm-weather months you can wear a strappy, open shoe, with a simple, sexier dress. Or you could wear a more basic but open shoe with a straight sheath-style dress in spring or summer.

If you're going to stray from traditional bridal shoes, make sure that they are either a white or bone leather that matches perfectly, or a fabric that can be dyed. I prefer peau de soie or other fabrics over leather, but if it's a perfect match and you love the shoes, go for it.

When it comes to dying shoes, you have more options than just matching a swatch of your dress identically. A perfect match is most popular, and quite appropriate. But you

Be daring and dress up your dyed-to-match silk pumps. Affix pearls or tiny silk rosettes with a hot glue gun, and you're in business.

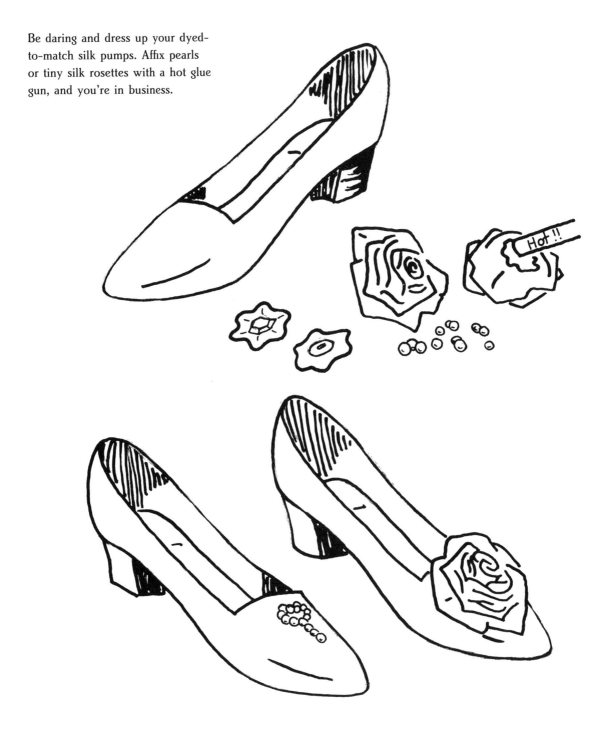

could also go with a very subtle tint. If you're wearing a really white wedding dress, a light-colored dusty pink shoe can be a nice accent. You can have your bridesmaids wear a dress in that very light shade, and perhaps have that color in your bouquet. It's a very subtle, elegant look that is highly coordinated.

But whether you choose to go the traditional route with shoes that match perfectly, or opt for more creative alternatives, it's important to give thought to the many footwear possibilities for your wedding day. It sometimes takes a bit of a search or an investigation to find the perfect shoes, but it's worth the trouble. All the shopping and trying on and practice-walking will fade from memory on your wedding day, when you take those fateful steps in shoes that ideally complete your look.

Your Hair . . . Managing Your Mane Like a Pro

5

MANY WOMEN HAVE HAD AN IMAGE OF THEM-selves as a bride in their minds for much of their lives. This vision often includes not just a certain kind of dress and headpiece but a particular hairstyle as well.

In the first chapter of this book, I recommended writing a paragraph about your vision of the important aspects of your wedding. If you haven't done this already, it's a good idea to include a sentence or two about what you want your hair to look like.

If you're going to have your hair done professionally for your wedding, or if you want to get your hair into good shape in time for the big day, I recommend paying a visit to a hairdresser almost as soon as you get engaged for a consultation about what your options are and advice on how to modify your current hairstyle. Hopefully, you have a hairdresser with whom you have a fairly long-standing relationship, and who knows your hair's texture and styles it well.

If you don't, I'd suggest finding one right away, through referrals from friends.

Once you have a hairdresser you're comfortable with, make sure he or she is available on your wedding day, and make the booking. Confirm this appointment as you get closer to the wedding.

On the day of the wedding, if you have decided to go to the hairdresser rather than having him or her come to you, be prepared for obstacles throughout and leading up to the appointment: traffic, weather, and other random time delays. I have found that a hair appointment always takes longer than you would expect. For a bride's hair and makeup to be done by one person, it will take approximately two and one half hours, and that doesn't include travel time. Ask your stylist to approximate the amount of time he or she will need so you can prepare accordingly. Try to have your hair and makeup done as close to your ceremony as possible so that they will remain fresh and hold for the six to eight hours ahead.

When you go for your consultation with your hairdresser just after you've gotten engaged, it's a good idea to bring along a Polaroid camera so that you can record whatever your hairdresser tries out and show it to other people. This is also a good idea if you plan to have a friend do your hair or do your hair by yourself. You can take step-by-step instructional photographs of the way the hairdresser places hot rollers in your hair and the way it gets pinned up. Bear in mind, though, that a hairstyle never looks exactly the same twice, even when it is done by a professional.

Whether or not you have always envisioned your hair a certain way for your wedding day, you will need to give consideration to your hair options early on, especially if, like many brides, you plan to grow your hair long for the wedding.

I come across this often in my salon work and my work with brides. As soon as a woman gets engaged, she'll say she wants to grow her hair out so that she can wear it either long or swept up for her wedding. Generally, a bride will come to me for a wedding consultation about eight months before her wedding, and if her hair is chin length or longer, long hair is an option.

I think a good style to work with in the months to a year that precede your wedding is a very simple haircut, which is chin length or longer, maybe with layers in the back and some cutouts around the front.

If you are determined to have long hair for your wedding, it is a good idea to start growing it out right away, although you should get a tiny trim—what I call a dusting—every three months or so, to keep the ends nice, to keep it healthy, and to keep whatever bit of style you have. But be sure to explain to your hairdresser that you want less cut off than you would have in a normal trim.

Bear in mind that most people's hair grows only about a half inch per month. Don't set yourself up for disappointment if your hair has a long way to go before it's the length you've always envisioned. You may have always pictured yourself having your hair cascading down your back, but be realistic about how much time you have, and try to alter your vision to reflect how long your hair can really be.

Then there are the brides who come in and ask whether it's okay to have short hair, and my answer is definitely yes. While I tend to prefer long hair, shorter styles can be just as natural, soft, and feminine, with a bit more sophistication.

If you have shortish hair and you want to wear it up for your wedding, you really don't have to grow it out too much. Your hair can easily be pinned up in a way that creates the illusion of longer tresses.

This versatile haircut is a great
baseline style for the bride-to-be.
The general shape works well for
straight chin-length or longer hair,
as well as for curly hair.

Layered, short hair tucked behind the ears is a great look for a modern bride.

Weather or Not

One very important factor in determining how you will wear your hair for your wedding is the time of year you're getting married, with relation to the texture of your hair. If you have naturally wavy or curly hair and you're planning to get married in June, July, or August, it's probably not a good idea to get your heart set on wearing your hair stick-straight. You can have your hair blown straight and swept up with pieces coming down. Those pieces will curl—but that can look quite pretty.

At the same time, if you have very thin, straight hair and you're getting married in the summertime, you have to try to find a way to make your hair look fuller and have more volume, so that it doesn't just stick flat to your head. (Refer to "The Tools of the Trade" beginning on page 86 for specific advice about products that can add volume to your hair.)

Fair Treatment

A few weeks before your wedding is *not* the time to begin experimenting with a new hairstyle, color, or perm. If you're thinking about making a change, either do it many months before so that you can make adjustments in time for your wedding, or wait until afterward.

If there are treatments that you regularly undergo, such as coloring, highlighting, or perming, you've got to formulate a plan about when to head for the hairdresser.

Women who color their hair should give some thought to when to get their coloring done. If you have single-process hair coloring to either dye your hair or cover up gray, be aware of your hair's growth pattern so that you can schedule an appointment that's not too close, but not too far from your wedding date. For example, if you're a woman who colors her hair every four to six weeks to cover up gray, make an appointment for a week or two before your wedding. You don't want to get your hair colored the day before, because sometimes the dye stains the skin around your hairline temporarily. You also don't want to do it a couple of days before, because the color tends to be unusually potent then; you'll wind up having that just-been-to-the-hairdresser color intensity look.

The same goes for highlighting, and touching up roots. Plan to get those redone a week or two before the wedding, even if it means holding off and having some roots showing for a few weeks before that. You want your coloring to look fresh for the wedding.

As for perming, if you have straight hair yet envision sporting great curls on your wedding day, but never permed your hair before, my advice is simple: Don't do it. I have never seen a perm work out the way a bride wished that it had. If you have a two-year engagement ahead of you, that's a different story. But even then, I'd recommend first just trying big hot rollers in your hair. Bangs also require special attention. They shouldn't be cut too close to the wedding, unless you want to look like Moe from the Three Stooges. The best time to have your bangs cut is probably two weeks beforehand.

If you have bangs and you want to grow them out in time for your wedding, get started on that as soon as you get engaged. It will require many awkward months of pinning them back with barrettes and bobby pins, or pushing them back with a headband, but it will pay off once your wedding day arrives.

A Matter of Style

How should your hair look for your wedding? Although there are certainly many different possibilities, my preference tends to be toward very simple, classic styles. Here are four tried-and-true options that work for many brides:

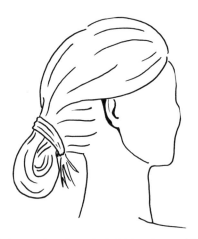

A loose, low knot is held in place with pins on the inside then tied with a strand of your own hair—which is then pinned and covered with a length of silk ribbon.

Barely shoulder-length hair is combed away from the face and flipped under neatly in the back.

Here's a more contemporary take on the shoulder-length theme—hair is parted low on the side and flipped up in the back.

A classic up-do with bangs

You might look through bridal magazines and find wonderfully elaborate hairdos. These can be very attractive, but if you're usually a no-fuss-type woman in your day-to-day grooming, you might feel awkward and not really look like yourself. Another disadvantage is that when that fancy hairstyle becomes dated, it will still be on view in your wedding pictures.

Funky changes for your wedding aren't really advisable either, for the same reasons. One bride I know, however, had fun dying her hair for her wedding, and it worked out. She and the groom coordinated in a rather unique way: He wore a pink tuxedo, and she dyed her hair to match it. It was very whimsical. There's really nothing wrong with being a funky bride; but I tend to favor a more traditional look.

It's your wedding day, and your dress and your headpiece will call enough attention to you. You don't also need to have an incredibly noticeable hairdo. No element of your ensemble should overpower another; everything should stay pretty much on the same level of sophistication, including your hairdo.

You have a number of choices, but I have a certain style of what I call classic wedding hair, which I think is most appropriate for brides who have hair that's chin length or longer, whether it's straight or curly, and whether or not you have bangs.

Whatever style you choose, if you are going to do it yourself or have someone close to you do your hair, make sure you schedule some practice runs. The key to any good hairstyle is practice. You should have at least one practice run or explicit conversation with your hairdresser to make sure you're both on the same wavelength.

I've learned from experience how important this is. One bride I worked with, Cristina, brought in pictures of the hairdo she wanted, which was very modern and trendy.

While she was in the salon with me, a few weeks before her wedding, I actually couldn't get the hairdo to work. I was so embarrassed. But Christina is a good friend, and she said she was sure I'd figure it out before the wedding. In the few weeks I had, I took the hairdo apart in my mind and actually tried it out on other friends until I got it right. Then, on Christina's wedding day, I was happy because I was able to bang out the hairdo she wanted, one-two-three. I couldn't believe how easy it had become.

Another bride I worked with, Katie, told me she didn't need to meet with me beforehand—I just had to show up at her hotel room on the morning of the wedding. I had been her hairdresser for years, and so she figured I'd be familiar enough with her hair and her taste. When I arrived that morning, we went over what she wanted verbally, and then I went to work creating my favorite wedding hairdo. When I was done, Katie asked me, "Is it going to be any higher?" I panicked, thinking she wasn't satisfied and I'd have to start over. Even though she wound up looking beautiful, it would have been better if we had worked out all the kinks in advance of Katie's wedding day.

That favorite hairdo I mentioned is a half-up, half-down style, in which the front pieces are tied back with a covered rubber band and the rest cascades down. A piece of hair is wrapped around the rubber band to give it a nice, finished look. Here's how you can create this style on your own.

My Favorite Classic Hairdo

  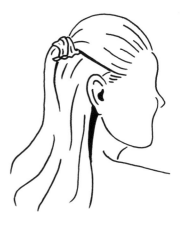

Step One: Pull hair from crown of head and lift into ponytail. Secure ponytail with coated ponytail holder.

Step Two: Wrap a piece of hair around the ponytail holder and secure underneath with bobby pins.

Step Three: Smooth hair behind ears for a finished look.

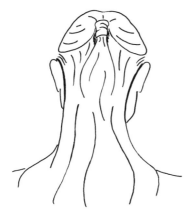

Back view

Profile view

Materials needed:

- ❧ Coated ponytail holder (preferably one that matches your color hair)
- ❧ 3–4 bobby pins
- ❧ hairbrush

Within this classic hair theme, there are a couple of variations:

❧ **If you have curly hair,** you might want to have one or two sizes of curling irons handy to put more definition into your curls. Or you might want to blow-dry your hair straight, if you're good at that, and then stack your hair with hot rollers for big, defined curls. There's also the option of letting your hair be kinky-curly, with frizz-free corkscrews, if that's your hair type. If you have access to a stationary dryer, this can work quite well.

I find this works best when you put a generous amount of product into the hair when it is damp, shape it with clips—which gives height in the front—and then sit under the dryer until the hair is 95 percent dry. This helps define the curl and reduce frizz. If you don't have access to a stationary dryer, purchase an inexpensive accessory called a diffuser that attaches to a blow dryer and acts as a dryer cap. Most professional hairdressers own these. Once your curls have been tamed, then you can create the classic hairdo.

❧ **Often, with this classic 'do, women want to create some height in their hair.** Creating height and getting it to stay can be a challenge. But I have formulated a way of doing it, by "building" what I have coined an "S-base" on the crown of the head. It is an S-shaped cushion made of your own hair on top of which you can then layer front pieces.

Here's how to create height with an S-base

Materials needed: ❧ *8–10 bobby pins;* ❧ *hairbrush*

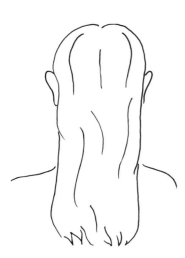

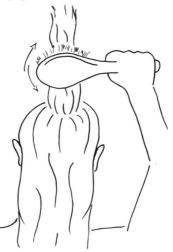

Step One: Start with hair brushed smoothly away from the face and tucked behind the ears.

Step Two: Take a one- or two-square-inch section of your hair just behind where you want the height in your hair and tease it upward from the root.

Step Three: Then bend that clump of hair into a loop that forms the shape of an "S."

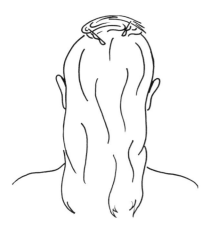

Step Four: Secure the "S" to your head with bobby pins. Don't worry—it doesn't have to be neat. No one is going to see it. This part of your hair is going to be covered up by the section of your hair in front of it, which will be swept over and held into place with pins.

Step Five: Take the section of hair directly in front of the S-base and bring it over the S-base. Secure with bobby pins.

Step Six: Anchor any hair to your S-base to create height and a smooth look. Keep in mind that the S-base also functions as a great foundation when you are mounting your headpiece and veil.

The Tools of the Trade

If you are not using a professional hairstylist on the day of your wedding and you or one of your friends plan to do your hair, it will help to know about certain tools and products that can help you create the look and texture you want. Remember—practice lots before the wedding day.

There are three main ingredients in the recipe for doing your hair: mousse, gel, and hair spray.

Mousse, in my mind, equals yeast. It correlates to baking: You don't need a lot of yeast to make bread rise very high, and you don't need a lot of mousse to create fullness. Both mousse and gel, in my opinion, are most effective when used with heat. If you are not going to use a blow-dryer, do not use either mousse or gel. If you are going to use these products, make sure you put them on only when your hair is damp.

If you have curly hair and you're going to wear it that way, take about a half dollar–sized dollop of mousse from a can into the palm of your hand. While your hair is damp, put your head upside down, and spread the mousse over every strand of your hair. The mousse will coat your hair, and let you create more consistent, tighter curls when you scrunch your hair and dry it with a blow-dryer.

Mousse can also provide volume for straight hair. Using a quarter-sized to a half dollar–sized dollop of mousse in your damp hair before blow-drying it upside down will get the roots to stand up a bit, away from your head, making your hair look really fuller.

Gel is something that I use primarily for the periphery of the hair, for a bit of height. If you put a bit of gel on your damp hair, only in the front area, in the first inch from your forehead, it will provide height around the front when you're blow-drying your hair. Also, the gel will help you blow the roots of your hair in the direction that you want. This is an important factor in getting your hair to go—and stay—the way you want it to.

Hair spray comes in two forms—pump and aerosol—and there's a big difference between the two. Aerosol sprays hurt the ozone layer, but they are really effective. Unfortunately, pump sprays tend to remoisten the hair. So, if you never use hair spray in an aerosol can again for as long as you live, make the exception and use it on your wedding day.

Hair spray doesn't usually come into play until the end of the styling process. But if you're going to use hot rollers, then you'll need to apply hair spray after your hair has been blown straight. You are going to use the hair spray on each section of hair that you put into rollers. You take the section you are about to roll and first spray it with aerosol hair spray. Then, quickly put a roller in. The hair spray will help you to keep the curl you create. By the way, when using rollers, always roll the hair in the direction *away* from the front of your head, from front to back.

There are some other products worth considering using on your hair, such as laminates and lotions—but be sure you try them out before your wedding day to get comfortable with them, and determine the amount your hair needs.

Laminates are oil-based products that are great for beating frizz and flyaways and adding shine. You use these after your hair is completely dry, whether you've just blown it dry or scrunched your curls.

Lotions, like Kiehl's Cream with Silk Groom and Paul

Mitchell's The Conditioner, are leave-in conditioners that have lanolin or cream bases. They're wonderful for eating frizz, too, and for giving a more polished look.

As for hardware, I think hot rollers are preferable to Velcro rollers, although Velcro ones can work well with aerosol hair spray. A curling iron really shouldn't be necessary, except if you want to put a major curl into straight hair and you're very comfortable using one.

How to Blow-Dry Your Hair

Before you approach rollers or any other styling tools, you need to blow-dry your hair. It's key that you blow it in such a way that it will create the effect you want, whether you want it straight and flat or full and curly, or loosely wavy.

I recommend blow-drying your hair hours before you're going to style it. This gives you time to relax with your wedding party and take care of other things while your hair smooths out or gets settled. **So here's the wedding day hair drill:**

1. Blow-dry your hair.
2. Put on your makeup (more about this in chapter 6).
3. Style your hair two hours before you're due to report for bridal duty.

For straight hair—step-by-step blow-dry tips: You probably want to create height and volume, so reach for mousse and/or a heat-activated gel like Redken's Centigrade. Using a Denman brush, a plastic brush which you can purchase at any drugstore, you'll begin working on the areas where you want height first.

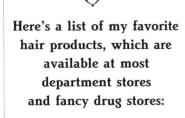

Here's a list of my favorite hair products, which are available at most department stores and fancy drug stores:

Paul Mitchell Sculpting Foam
Redken Centigrade Gel
Sebastian Shaper Plus Hair Spray
Kiehl's Cream with Silk Groom
Paul Mitchell Seal and Shine
Phytodefrisant (hair straightening balm)
Behr Naked Mousse
Behr Naked Shine Serum
(For these last two products, see page 169 for ordering instructions.)

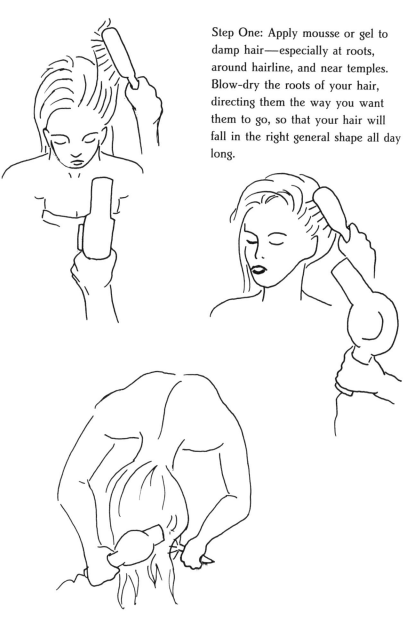

Step One: Apply mousse or gel to damp hair—especially at roots, around hairline, and near temples. Blow-dry the roots of your hair, directing them the way you want them to go, so that your hair will fall in the right general shape all day long.

Step Two: Next, toss your head upside down and brush your hair away from your head while blow-drying. Blowing your hair upside down creates a lot of volume.

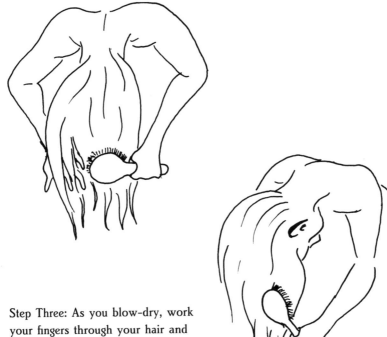

Step Three: As you blow-dry, work
your fingers through your hair and
lift hair from the roots with your
brush.

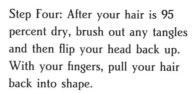

Step Four: After your hair is 95 percent dry, brush out any tangles and then flip your head back up. With your fingers, pull your hair back into shape.

Step Five: Now that your hair is mostly dry, you can begin to style it with a round brush. The pieces in front of your hair, whether they are small cutouts or long pieces, will look best with some "bend" (stylist lingo for shape) in them. Use a smaller round brush for this purpose. The secret to using a round brush is to leave it in place for a moment after you've taken away the heat, to let the cool air lock in the bend. Heat puts the bend in; cool air keeps it in place.

Step Six: Smooth hair into place— you've just blown-dry your hair like a pro. Consider using a few hot or Velcro rollers to create additional curl.

> **Must-have hair tools:**
>
> Clairol Kindness velvet-coated hot rollers
>
> Mason Pearson junior-size brush
>
> Denman brush (looks like a brush, works like a comb)
>
> Two mixed-bristle round brushes in one-inch and two-inch sizes
>
> Solis Heat Controlled Blow Dryer
>
> Velcro rollers in one-, two-, and three-inch sizes
>
> Portable dryer hood that attaches to your blow-dryer
>
> Beauty supply store hairpins and bobby pins (make a *big* difference)

For curly hair—step-by-step blow-dry tips: Keep in mind that you want to use a blow-dry method that avoids creating frizz. Apply mousse or gel to damp hair, especially at roots, around hairline, and near temples. First, you'll want to blow-dry the roots to get them to go in the direction you want. You can use your Denman brush around the perimeter of your scalp to create height and pull the roots of your hair away from your face. Do not pull the brush through the length of your hair; only dry the roots. Then move on to what I call the step-by-step "scrunching" process:

Whatever way you choose to wear your hair, remember that you'll need to pay extra attention to styling on your wedding day, as compared to your daily grooming routine. Get comfortable with the idea of using more hair product than you're accustomed to, and make sure you—or someone in your wedding party—are comfortable fixing your hair. On your wedding day, your hairdo needs to stay in place for a long time and look precise and neat. It's the hairdo you'll remember for the rest of your life.

Step One: Turn your head upside down and blow-dry sections of your hair scrunched close to your head in the palm of your hand. Keep your blow-dryer on a low setting.

Step Two: Remove the heat while the hair is still scrunched and let the cool air lock the curl in your hand before letting go. Take your time. Repeat this process until your hair is 95 percent dry.

Step Three: Flip your head back up. If you have lots of curly ringlets and you want to pile them on top of your head allowing a few curls to cascade down, scrunch for as much volume as possible. Then you can pin your hair up to the crown of your head in small sections—after first creating an S-base with sturdy pins from a beauty supply store.

Let's Make Up . . .
A Step-by-Step Approach
to Bridal Beauty

6

W E ALL WANT TO WEAR OUR BEST FACE ON THE day of our wedding, both literally and figuratively. Being properly prepared to put on your makeup on your wedding day is a big help—your makeup will look better, and you'll be more radiant because you'll be more confident.

No, putting on your wedding makeup is not simply a matter of just getting up that morning and doing your usual routine with foundation, mascara, blush, and lipstick. Your wedding day is going to be recorded in photographs and very likely on videotape, so it's important to pay more attention to your makeup, and certainly not just on the big day.

In fact, the preparation for your wedding day makeup should begin weeks, even months before. You need to get your skin ready for your wedding. Good, healthy skin means you'll need less makeup, and the makeup you do wear will work with your complexion more compatibly.

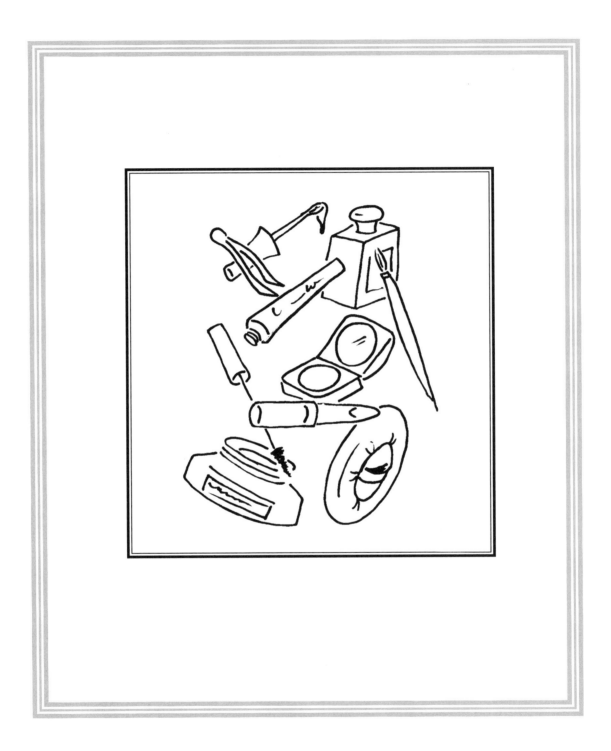

It isn't too soon to begin a healthy skin regimen even two months before your wedding. If you frequently wear foundation and other makeup, chances are your skin isn't completely even and healthy. It will need time to reneutralize itself. While you might not be comfortable leaving the house without foundation because your skin is a bit blotchy, it's a good idea to bite the bullet and wear either no makeup or less for a while. Your skin will improve gradually, and within a twenty-one-day period, it should be totally reneutralized.

It will help to get on a good skin regimen of cleansing and moisturizing, and getting plenty of that beauty sleep your mother always talked about. You can take a very basic, at-home approach:

1. Cleanse your face with Neutragena soap, which is mild and works for all types of skin.
2. Twice a week, exfoliate with a simple oatmeal-and-water scrub that you can whip up in your kitchen. The recipe is simple: Mix ½ cup of oatmeal with ¼ cup of lukewarm water until a coarse paste is formed. Rub onto skin gently, then rinse with warm water.
3. Apply an egg-white mask once a week. Separate one egg and lightly beat white with a fork. Slather on your face, leave on for fifteen minutes, then rinse with warm water.
4. Use a light moisturizer after each cleansing routine.

A professional facial at a salon can clear your skin, and if you choose to do that, your appointment should take place several days before your wedding because facials can cause temporary blemishing. If you have problem skin, plan to go to a dermatologist a month or so before your wedding, perhaps to start a cycle of antibiotics for acne treatment. If you do clear up your skin, keep in mind that it will need time to heal, dry, and then exfoliate or peel before the formerly blemished area is the same texture as the rest of your skin.

You'll want to take care of any bleaching, plucking, waxing, or electrolysis on your face about two weeks before your wedding. Remove hair or the sight of it fairly close to the wedding so that it's really exact, but not so close that it might interfere with the way your skin is going to look. Know your hair growth pattern and how long it will take for any resulting redness or bleeding to disappear.

In the months before your wedding, pay attention to the shape of your eyebrows. Keep in mind that the better defined your eyebrows are, believe it or not, the less makeup you will need to wear. You don't want to look overplucked or overshaped, but you want to create a refined shape that frames your eyes. With good, clear skin and a good eyebrow shape, you're way ahead of the game.

How to Shape Your Eyebrows

Eyebrow plucking is a tricky business. We've all seen women who've plucked too much, then attempted to draw in brows unevenly. In shaping your brows, your goal is to look natural yet streamlined. Be careful! Don't try to pluck your brows for the first time the night before the wedding. So this several weeks—months, even—before your wedding to allow time for regrowth if necessary.

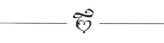

The Suntan Rule

Basking in the sun on your honeymoon is great, but tanning before the wedding is an absolute no-no. A tan bride not only photographs poorly, but the contrast of her skin tone with her dress and other (paler) members of her bridal party is too dramatic and unflattering. A healthy glow is okay. But no baking.

Here's an easy-to-follow formula for cleaning up your brows:

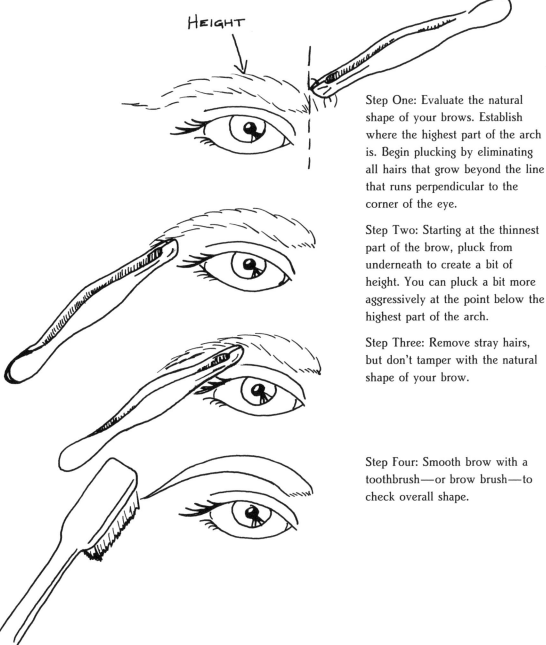

HEIGHT

Step One: Evaluate the natural shape of your brows. Establish where the highest part of the arch is. Begin plucking by eliminating all hairs that grow beyond the line that runs perpendicular to the corner of the eye.

Step Two: Starting at the thinnest part of the brow, pluck from underneath to create a bit of height. You can pluck a bit more aggressively at the point below the highest part of the arch.

Step Three: Remove stray hairs, but don't tamper with the natural shape of your brow.

Step Four: Smooth brow with a toothbrush—or brow brush—to check overall shape.

Try, Try Again

Don't even think of doing your own makeup on your wedding day without first practicing beforehand. A few trial runs will help you figure out how you look best. And remember, on your wedding day, and probably during your practice runs, you'll want to wear a button-down shirt so that you can change afterward without smudging everything. Also, be sure to do your tries and the final run in good, natural light that's not too bright or glaring.

Before you get started on one of your practice makeup sessions, first determine what style of makeup you're going to wear. I personally prefer and recommend a very natural style of makeup that simply enhances your features. For more formal weddings, you might want your makeup to be a little glamorized, but that glamour should be very subtle— you shouldn't look as if you're going to a black-tie New Year's Eve party. Dramatic, smoky eyes and scarlet lips are not appropriate when you're the bride.

Next, you'll want to get your skin in great condition that day—whether it's for one of your trials or the actual day. Your skin must be immaculate—no flakes of yesterday's mascara, no hint of a line from last evening's eyeliner. Make sure your pores are closed and your skin is moisturized, and coat your lips with a lip balm like Chap Stick or a vitamin E and aloe vera stick. Before you can begin, you need a good canvas.

Lastly, think about the season of your wedding. If the weather is going to be warm and the reception is held outdoors, and you tend to perspire, do not plan to wear lots of foundation, because foundation will not survive a sweaty bride. If you're getting married in the dead of winter, and

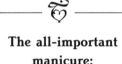

The all-important manicure:

I think that medium-length nails are appropriate, not only for your wedding day but for every day. Excessive length not only looks distracting and garish, but long talons can be dangerous on your wedding day when lots of people are lunging toward you for hugs and kisses.

As for nail color, lean toward sheer hues in light pastels and neutrals, like baby pinks, creams, and light taupes. A French manicure can look nice, although wearing a simple sheer shade on a well-manicured hand is the more elegant choice.

With a clean, fresh face, you can now begin your practice makeup routine.

Hot weather survival tip

On a humid, sunny day, wearing less makeup is the way to go. You'll most likely become flushed from the weather, so adding foundation and blush will only make you look (and feel) sweaty, sticky, and overheated. Keep a cotton handkerchief and your loose powder and puff close at hand to blot any perspiration or shininess.

A few favorite makeup products:

MAC eyeshadows—in Picadilly, Quarry, Yogurt, and Form

Il Makiage blush—in Cantaloupe and Spumoni

Maybelline Stick Concealer

Maybelline Great Lash Mascara

Kiehl's Lip Balm

The Behr Naked Makeup Pouch (my hands-down favorite—see page 169 for ordering instructions)

your skin gets dry, make sure you moisturize, moisturize, moisturize. And keep your lips moist, too. Otherwise, every line in your face, every flake of dry skin, will be amplified by your foundation and your powder.

Step by Step by Step . . .

Things You'll Need—Makeup Essentials for the Beautiful Bride.

Most of the following products can be purchased at your local drugstore. They need not be very expensive, and you should do an inventory of what you have at home before rushing out to buy all new stuff.

Lip balm

Moisturizer

Foundation that matches your complexion perfectly

A lighter foundation to use as concealer

Loose powder

Two pointy, wedged makeup sponges

A powder puff

Two big, fluffy makeup brushes for blending and applying loose powder and blush

One small, thick makeup brush for applying eye shadow

One thin, flat, small makeup brush for applying eyeliner

One small, thick, pointed makeup brush for blending eye shadow

An eyelash curler

A safety pin or an eyelash comb

A toothbrush

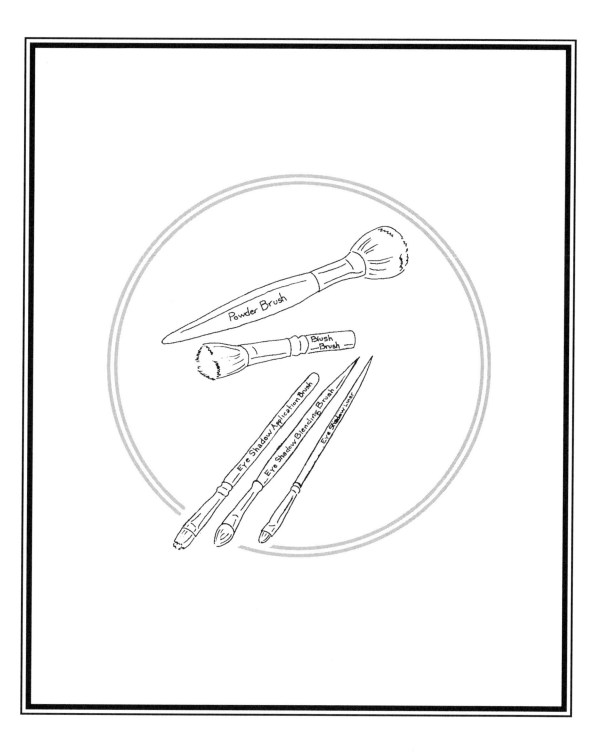

Mascara

Eye shadow—two shades of brown and one creamy ivory shade

Blush in a pale peachy color

Lip liner in a brown-based shade of pink or red

Lipstick

Q-Tips

Tissues

The Makeup Routine:

First things first: Lay out all your products and tools in front of you for your makeup tries, and ultimately for your wedding day, so you don't have to go fishing through your makeup case and spill things, then suddenly discover you've run out of something.

Once your tools are laid out before you and your canvas is ready—your skin and lips are moisturized—you can begin to apply the first layer. It begins with concealer, which doesn't necessarily mean a product that is labeled that way. I find that stick concealer tends to be gummy and comes off easily. I also find that it often makes lines and circles under eyes look worse, and so I never use it on women over thirty, unless I'm trying to cover up a red spot or blemish. If you are going to use a standard concealer, though, my favorite is Maybelline's concealer stick, in the lightest shade available.

If you need to conceal lines and circles, I recommend choosing a foundation that's a shade lighter than your regular foundation—which should be the same color as your skin, or a shade lighter, not darker, if you are white skinned. You could use a color like porcelain or ivory for your concealer, for example, and cream beige as your foundation color. I recommend choosing oil-based, liquid foundation for both. An oil-based foundation is not as pore clogging and acne inviting as some people might think. It's whipped and glides on very smoothly, and works with the oils in your skin to seep in rather than sitting caked on top of your face.

Take your concealer and dab it on with either a wedged sponge that is not mealy, or with your fingers. The point of the sponge will allow you to get into nooks and crannies, like the edges of your nostrils, easily.

Apply your concealer or lighter shade of foundation in dab-type spots on any areas you want to be evened with your skin. Go from the center of the spot you want to erase, and then blend going outward from that spot. If you're erasing darker circles/bags under your eyes, try to remember to conceal your entire eye. It is not just the portion underneath your eye. Bring it all the way from the base underneath your eyelashes toward the side of your nose, to the very top of your cheek, and all the way to the side of the bone of your eye. And blend, blend, blend—down and out.

Once your concealer layer has been absorbed into your skin for about a minute or so, it's time to apply your foundation. Even if you don't need to wear foundation because you have wonderful skin, you'll still need to wear it at least on your eyelids, up to your eyebrows, so that any makeup or eye shadow can adhere to your skin.

Make sure your foundation is shaken and at room temperature. Take a dime-size amount into the hand you're not using to apply the makeup. With either your hand or makeup sponge, start at your cheekbone, work up toward your eye, and blend one side of the face and then the other. You start with a dime-size amount because you don't want to wear a lot of makeup. Glide it on your face so that your face is covered with this moisturized layer of foundation. Blending is important. If you need more, add another dime-size portion to the hand you're not using. The foundation must seep into every crack in your face, and every edge. Blend it down so it blends into your neckline.

With a clean sponge or a clean finger, go over the whole surface very lightly and pick up the excess foundation that did not absorb, and this will help to blend and make your skin color and the foundation color become one even tone. Then do the same with a clean tissue and blot your entire face to absorb oil and excess foundation.

Rest for about thirty seconds before moving on to the loose powder. This is not a compact powder. It's something you can buy anywhere. Your choice has to do with your skin tone. You have to choose between pink or yellow undertones. The majority of Caucasian and light-skinned women look best in powder with a yellow undertone. If you're an "Ivory girl," you might go more toward a pink-toned powder. If you have any ethnicity and have light- to medium-toned skin, you should probably wear a yellow-toned powder. But it doesn't matter that much because the powder essentially disappears. The purpose of the powder is simply to seal in your foundation and even out your skin.

Take your powder puff and put a fair to generous amount on it. Lightly pat your face everywhere—your nose, your eyelids, underneath your eyes, your chin. You'll actually apply quite a bit of powder on your face. Then take a very soft, large makeup brush and brush off all the remaining powder, so that no visible powder is left on your face. At this point you should see a more even, paler version of yourself. What should stand out now are your moistened lips and your eye (iris) color, because you've neutralized your features and taken a lot of color away from your face.

Wait another thirty seconds—a big part of making your makeup look good is giving your face time during the process to absorb the makeup. Make sure your hands are not moist or perspiring and slowly take your fingers to your face, push in all the powder, and let it seep into your skin. The warmth from your hands will allow that to happen.

If any blemishes still stand out, take your concealer and dab those spots again without blending too much. Leave it alone for a while.

Depending on your coloring, your eyebrows might not need more than a good shaping. But if you have pale skin and light hair, then consider using eyebrow pencil. If you're a woman with dark eyebrows, the brow shape alone with no pencil is perfect. If you're a woman with light brown or blond eyebrows, find an eyebrow pencil in the brown family. I look for brown and blond. Blond pencils tend to look a little taupe, but they look very good on light skin and hair. Some people prefer eyebrow powder, but I don't think it works as well; you don't have as much control over it. If you're going to darken your eyebrows, I think pencil is better.

When you start penciling your eyebrows, stay within the shape of the natural brow. Do not start by drawing on new eyebrows. Take your pencil and start with the eyebrow base, the thickest part closest to your nose. With short quick strokes, go up and follow the line that is already there. Most people have the most difficulty with the end of the eyebrow at the outside of your eye, where it's the most faint. It should be the thinnest part, and the line should go out and down, not just down. This is something you should certainly practice if you don't normally do it.

Next, take a toothbrush and brush your eyebrow to blend your pencil into the eyebrow. Then take a Q-Tip and go above and below the eyebrow to take away any excess pencil that has extended beyond your actual eyebrow. The pencil should only appear in the hairs of your eyebrow.

Finally, take the loose powder puff and dab some powder on your eyebrows to set them. Then take your powder brush and brush away—lightly—any excess powder.

You're ready to begin applying eye shadow. There are two different approaches—one for light-skinned women with larger eyelids, and one for those with smaller lids. In each case, I recommend having three powdered eye shadow colors on hand: *creamy ivory, light brown or pale pink*, and a slightly *darker brown*. For women with larger eyelids, the darker brown will play a different role than it will for women with smaller eyelids, but in each case, its main function will be to enhance and emphasize what you already have—not to paint on new eyes.

Step One: First you're going to apply the color that's going to go on your eyelid. For women with larger lids, this color should be the lighter brown color so that it looks natural or pale pink. Women with smaller eyes can use either the darker or the lighter brown to shade their eyelids; a darker color can sometimes be a nice backdrop for your pupil color if you have small eyes.

This main color should be generously applied to the

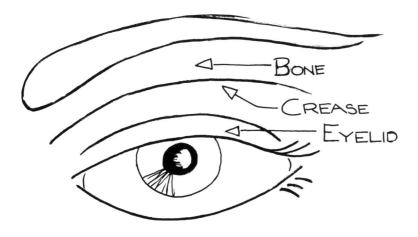

BONE
CREASE
EYELID

eyelid, in a round motion, reaching but not covering the base of the brow bone. You can apply it with a flat, thick brush. Bring it all the way down to the eyelashes, but not in too close to where your nose starts. Take another fluffier brush, and blend the color in that area.

Step Two: Next comes the creamy ivory color. This color highlights the space between the brow and the lid. It acts as a footlight in your photography, opening up your eye. You want to apply that color almost completely around the outer edges of the eyelid, from the base of your eyebrow, down toward the outside of your eye.

Step Three: Here's where another distinction is made with regard to eye size. Women with larger eyelids should take the darker brown color and apply it along the crease of the eye. To be sure of where that is, open your eyes wide, take a pointy brush and follow the curve of the crease. Take the pointier, longer, softer brush and blend the darker color down, into the lighter color on the lid, so your eye will have depth behind it. You can also use that darker brown as an eyeliner.

For women with smaller eyelids, if you've chosen to

Finding the right lipstick can be tough. Here's my list of favorite hues for brides:

Il Makiage—New Ginger lip pencil

Max Factor—Rose Dusk and Carmine Pink

L'Oréal—True Rose 606 and Tendre Mauve 524

Revlon—Cocoa Wine #16 and Soft Shell #88

Cover Girl—Bronzed Glow and Shimmering Shell

Prescriptives—Shell (neutral light pink) and Tube Rose (brown base with rose)

Clinique—Angel Red, Classic Red, and Tender Heart (natural)

MAC—Viva Glam 1 (brown/red), Viva Glam 2 (light pink), and Mocha (neutral)

Chanel—Beige de Chanel #2 (lightly frosted cream)

Origins—Adobe #16 (brown base with orange tint) and Creamsickle #41 (pale, sheer peach)

Lancôme—Coquette (pearlized mauve-y pink) and Rose Nu (medium pink/red)

Makeup no-no's

- Orange or excessively dark lipstick . . . These colors look severe on a day when you want to look subtle.

- Liquid eyeliner . . . Again, the effect is too dramatic and severe. This is not a night on the town; it's your wedding. Also, you may be crying and most likely perspiring, and the moisture will make your liner run.

- Full sets of false eyelashes . . . Adding a few individual lashes is okay, but a full set will never look natural. Avoid these, unless you want to look like Liza Minelli on your wedding day.

continued

use a lighter brown as your main color, you can also use the darker brown as an eyeliner.

Step Four: I prefer using shadow as an eyeliner. It's much more subtle than pencil, and it's also easier to use if you're not comfortable drawing a straight line across your eyelid. Shadow requires blending, as opposed to drawing.

To apply shadow as an eyeliner, take a brush that's very thin and flat and dab it into the darker brown color. Pull your eye back so that the eyelash base is showing. Make a line that extends all the way across the eyelash base. Then take the lighter-colored shadow on the same thin, flat brush and use it to outline underneath your eye, very close to your bottom lashes. Take it all the way around your eye. Take another Q-Tip and move it in a rolling motion to pick up any powder that has fallen on the outer areas.

Your eyelashes are next in line. Before you apply your mascara, curl your eyelashes with an eyelash curler. This will help to open your eye just a little bit more. If you don't often use an eyelash curler, get comfortable with it first. Make sure you don't pinch your eyelid skin with it. Count to twenty and lift. But be sure to open the curler before you pull it away.

When it comes to selecting a mascara color, I recommend black or brown—both shades are so similar, it doesn't make that much difference which one you choose. I suggest that if you're blond you use brown, but black can work in a pinch. Maybelline Great Lash mascara is my favorite brand.

I personally don't think waterproof mascara is necessary. If you make a mistake with it, it's really hard to fix it. Also, when you cry, it tends to come off your eyelashes but stick to your skin.

When you take the wand out of the tube, be sure to

brush off a lot of the excess mascara. It's easier to put a second coat on than to separate gooey lashes. And, as with everything, less is more. Slowly start from the base of the top lashes and coat your lashes going up. Don't forget about the lashes closest to your nose and at the edges of your eyes. Move the brush back and forth a little bit to keep the lashes as separated as possible. Then take an open safety pin and carefully separate your lashes. You can also use an eyelash comb. If you want more drama, put on a second coat, and emphasize the lashes on either edge.

There should be very little mascara left on the wand at this point. Now, if you want, you can very lightly brush your lower eyelashes. They look best when not coated in a noticeable fashion.

Now that you have your canvas of foundation and your eyes done, it is time to add color to your face—in moderation. I find that Caucasian women look good in "peaches-and-cream" colors, which can be pinky or cantaloupey, in combination. Dark-skinned and African-American women tend to look best in different shades of plummy, violet colors.

Combine both colors—pink and cantaloupe or plum and violet—on a fluffy round makeup brush. Find your cheekbone, smile, and start at the apple of your cheek and work your way up to your temple, but do not blend the color toward your eye, or the lower part of your cheek. Keep the blush in the cheekbone area. Dust your makeup brush in a circular motion. If you want to create with a darker blush, keep a light touch. Do not get carried away with contour. If you're light skinned, use a light, taupey color. If you're dark skinned, look for a rich, plummy color. This contour color should go under your cheekbone.

- Dark nail polish . . . Colors like Chanel's Vamp are very mod for every day, but your wedding is special, and you don't want to look trendy.
- Self-tanner . . . Tan-in-a-bottle streaks unevenly and can give you an other-worldly orange glow.
- Dark lip liner with a lighter lipstick . . . This combo is out of style, unattractive, and a definite *no*.

Also, dab your chin, the tip of your nose, and the center of your forehead with your lighter blushes.

Now take your powder puff and blend the color in the same area and the same motion, going up toward your temple from the apple of your cheek. Pat your chin, pat your nose, pat your forehead. Your face will have a glow to it.

You're ready to do your lips. I prefer lipsticks with a neutral brown base. You can go toward the red family, the pink family, or stay in the neutral family. I don't like orange colors on brides, or plums.

Do not apply your lipstick until after your dress is on. You may, however, start with your lip pencil, which is close in color to your lipstick.

Make sure your lips are moist but not gooey. Kiss off any excess balm. Take your lip pencil color, which will actually act as the base coat for your lipstick, and start in the center of your upper lip. Draw a "V" in the center of your upper lip, then line your lip. Next, start at the base of your lower lip, and trace it. Try and emphasize your lips—draw a line with your pencil just outside the contour of your lips. You'll be sure to want to try this out *before* the wedding day. Use your pencil to fill in the rest of your lips. Rub your lips together. Then take your makeup sponge that has very little foundation or concealer on it, and touch up the edges. Make sure that the line around your lips is pretty exact.

Finish it all off. Shake most of the loose powder off your large makeup brush, and dust your face, except for your lips. This will seal everything in, and you'll be all made up for your wedding day. Of course, you haven't yet applied your lipstick—you'll do so after your dress is on and your hair is finished.

Flowery Sentiments . . . Selecting Flowers for Yourself and Your Wedding Party

7

O F ALL THE DETAILS A BRIDE TENDS TO WHEN PLAN-
ning her wedding, flowers are often the issue she
knows the least about. In choosing a bridal bouquet—as well as flowers for your attendants, your parents,
the groom, and the groomsmen—you might need to do a
little research. So few people are really knowledgeable about
different types of flowers and what's available in certain
regions at certain times of year.

One very good way to start your research is to look at
garden magazines and floral magazines—not because they'll
have bouquet designs but because you can see a variety of
flowers and learn their names, and learn enough about them
to figure out whether they'll be available for your wedding.

Once you've familiarized yourself a little bit with different types of flowers, you might want to glance at some British and Australian bridal magazines for ideas about bouquet
designs. Those magazines tend to have a much more simple

Brides Beware!

The flowers you carry on your
wedding day will be wet on the
bottom. Don't make the mistake
of taking them directly from the
box in which the florist has sent
them and bringing them up
against your gown. You'll wind
up with a big water stain on the
front of your dress. I've seen this
happen way too many times.
Have someone first check the
base of the bouquet before you
grab it. Pass this tip along to
your bridesmaids, too.

Long-stemmed French tulips
wrapped in a silk ribbon: Is this
your bouquet?

and elegant sensibility than American bridal magazines. In fact, they're good to check out, in general, for planning your wedding, because they're beautiful magazines, filled with great style concepts.

When choosing your own bridal flowers, keep in mind that you want to reflect the tone of your wedding, whether it's modern or traditional. One very traditional concept is for the bride to carry all roses, in a variety of shades of white and cream. In contrast, your bridesmaids could be carrying roses closer to the tones of the dresses they're wearing, such as light pinks or creamy yellows. The groom and all the groomsmen could then wear a variation on the theme of roses on their lapels: small roses, baby roses, large roses, antique roses, all in a similar color palette.

You also want to think about the time of year and the setting. Your flowers should coordinate with the mood of the venue and should have an appropriate feel if your wedding is taking place in a church or temple, or in a dark, wood-paneled library, or in a summer garden setting, where you might consider having multiple colors in your bouquets because there are so many vibrant flowers available. The same goes for the flowers you choose as centerpieces.

And while your bouquet and your bridesmaids' bouquets shouldn't exactly match the centerpieces, they should coordinate with all the flowers throughout the wedding. There should be one cohesive floral concept.

As a bride, you'll have to decide whether to carry long-stemmed flowers or a bouquet. It's a big decision. I happen to prefer a bouquet for the bride. In my opinion, carrying long-stemmed flowers while walking down the aisle is a little bit Miss America-ish. I also think it can be uncomfortable to carry long-stemmed flowers, although a bouquet of flowers isn't exactly the most natural thing for you to hold, either.

The dress/bouquet connection

Different types of dresses call for different types of personal bouquets:

With a modern sheath or shift-type dress, choose a longer-stemmed flower, like a calla lily.

With a traditional full-skirted dress, choose a tight bouquet with spilling vines.

With a Vera Wang–type dress that has clean, classic lines, choose a closely arranged bouquet of cream and white antique roses.

Roses—all in shades of white and
cream—make a rich bouquet for
the traditional bride.

Whatever you choose, your flowers should definitely be grander than the bouquets carried by other attendants in the wedding party. *Grander* doesn't necessarily mean *larger*. It means the bride's flowers should either be fuller, or more detailed, or more varied in color, and certainly not the same as the bridesmaids' and maid of honor's bouquets.

Similarly, the groom's boutonniere should definitely be different from his best man's and the groomsmen's. It shouldn't necessarily be larger, but it might have an extra detail. For example, if roses are the floral theme for the wedding, the groom might wear one large rose with two baby roses underneath it, and the groomsmen might just have a cluster of baby roses on their lapels.

In addition to carrying flowers, some brides also choose to incorporate flowers into their ensemble, wearing them in their hair. When it comes to wearing flowers in your hair, heed the rule that also applies to accessories and makeup: Less is more. And while many people tend to gravitate toward baby's breath, I think it's preferable to choose live flowers rather than dried ones, when there are so many wonderful options.

Choose very small, delicate flowers if you're going to wear them in your hair at all. The same goes for your bridesmaids. The flowers in their hair should be very similar to the ones they're carrying, only much, much smaller. Again, as I mentioned in the veil and headpiece chapter, wearing flowers in your hair looks beautiful, but it's difficult to secure flowers to your hairdo so that they last all day or all evening long. Have a professional hairstylist—or a skilled member of your wedding party—do this for you.

Flower don'ts

- Don't thread baby's breath throughout your hair.
- Don't place a flower behind your ear.
- Don't select personal flowers that seem out of sync with the rest of the flowers chosen for your wedding.
- Don't walk down the aisle like a beauty queen holding three long-stemmed red roses.

Create a romantic—and portable—
nosegay with a mixture of
Canterbury bells and miniature ivy.

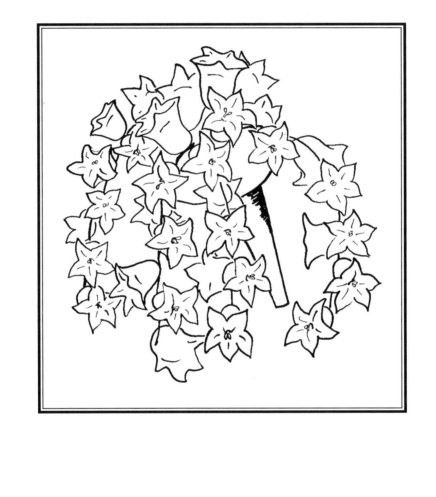

The modern yet chic alternative:
Bind the long stems of six or seven
calla lilies with a thick silk cord
that matches your dress.

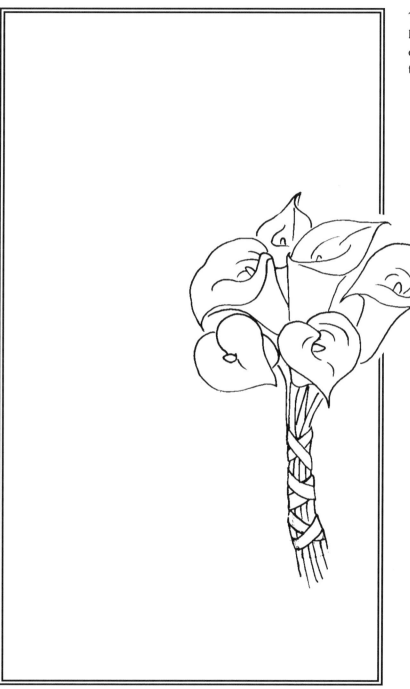

Members of the Wedding . . . A Special Course in Bridesmaid Beauty

8

AT LEAST ONCE IN THEIR LIVES, MOST BRIDES HAVE been a bridesmaid in someone else's wedding. If you've walked in a bridesmaid's or maid of honor's shoes before, you know that the experience can be a mixed blessing: While it's a special honor and a compliment to be invited into someone's wedding party, it's also a financial burden, a bit of work—and a potential fashion nightmare.

Your own wedding is a great opportunity to create for your attendants the bridesmaid experience you have always wished for. There are so many ways to help your close friends and relatives look beautiful and feel welcome.

Some women equate being asked to be in a wedding party with being asked to wear an ugly, cumbersome, flamboyant dress. But now there are many more beautiful dress options than in the past. There is no longer any reason why a woman has to look like Scarlett O'Hara at someone else's wedding.

But regardless of how pretty or sophisticated your choice of bridesmaids' dresses may be, do yourself and your attendants a favor: Don't tell them they can wear the dress again. Maybe the dress is elegant and basic enough that they can, but the truth is, they probably won't. Anyone who requires that sort of a rationalization shouldn't be in your wedding party in the first place.

Where to Begin

If you are going to shop for bridesmaids' dresses in an old-fashioned bridal shop or the bridal department of a larger store, you are likely to find the typical, cliché bridesmaid dress—a thick, taffeta floral print dress with pleats and a big bow in the back. Let's just say that this is far from ideal. The goal is not just to have your bridesmaids match, at any cost.

A better place to begin might be the evening gown department of your local department store. There is a wide array of beautiful dresses in these departments that would be appropriate for an evening wedding. If you're getting married in the summer, you'll find a broad range of dresses designed to be worn for proms and graduation parties available around April, and many of these will be good options.

Yes, bridesmaids' dresses can be bought off the rack. They needn't be handmade, although that's still an alternative. Remember, even celebrities buy beautiful evening dresses off the rack. There are a lot of great dresses for reasonable prices out there.

Don't be afraid to use your department store as a resource. If a particular store doesn't have all the dresses you need, ask them to order more, in the sizes you're looking for.

When it comes to outfitting bridesmaids, these dress designers really know their stuff:

Nicole Miller
Vera Wang
Bill Levkoff
Vivienne Tam
Cynthia Rowley
(See the Resource list on page 164 for information on how to locate these labels at stores near you.)

A great off-the-rack bridesmaid's dress from a department store.

They can have them shipped from other branches, or from the manufacturer.

Always a Bridesmaid

Because your wedding party brings together a number of diverse personalities, including people from two different families, you are bound to be inundated with varying opinions about the dresses, on everything from the color, to the fabric, to the length. That's why I recommend first going and looking for dresses by yourself—do not even bring along your maid of honor. Go to a department store and see what is available in terms of styles and prices.

As you browse, keep in mind each of your bridesmaids' personal concerns. Take money into consideration, and be sensitive to your bridesmaids' budgets. If you feel the need to be insistent on something, be prepared to be incredibly generous with your own money, and don't give anyone a guilt trip about it. It's your wedding. Be generous if you want a woman to be a bridesmaid who can't afford it.

These are your closest friends and female relatives. You know them the way you know yourself. Consider whether they'll be comfortable with their arms showing, whether there's someone who's especially busty or flat chested who might feel uneasy in a body-revealing dress.

If most of your bridesmaids are thin and shapely, but one or two are a little more heavyset, a nice thing to do is to have chiffon wraps made to match the dresses. They can be easily crafted by a friend or relative—or a tailor—by taking lengths of chiffon that are twice the height of each bridesmaid, doubling them over, and sewing a half-inch seam around the entire rectangle. Presenting these to them in a

Bridesmaids' dresses need not always be long. With shorter styles, make sure that everyone's panty hose and shoes coordinate perfectly.

This long bridesmaid's dress is tasteful—and a flattering bet for most body types.

nice box as a bridesmaid's gift makes them special, while sensitively addressing your attendants' desires to cover up.

Alternative Options

If you're a bride who has bridesmaids of extremely different sizes and tastes, you may not feel right just choosing one dress and telling everyone to purchase it. There are other ways to create a uniform look for your bridal party without everyone wearing the exact same dress. And it may be for the best.

One option is to just choose a color and length, and let your bridesmaids choose any dress of their liking. This option tends to work best with black, because with other colors there are too many varying shades.

But beware: A bride who lets everyone choose her own style gets involved in a lot of extra footwork. She needs to go with each bridesmaid to make sure all the dresses look harmonious together. And that's a huge responsibility.

One bride I know had a bridal party filled with women of different shapes and sizes. She addressed this by choosing a fabric and three dress patterns that flattered different shapes. She found a seamstress who would make any of three patterns for each bridesmaid for about $200. And everyone was happy.

Another bride I know told her bridesmaids to go to the department store and get any style of black dress by the same designer, as long as it was a certain length. Choosing one designer ensures that there will be similar tailoring on the dresses, and that there will be some degree of coordination.

> ❧
> ### Synchronicity counts
>
> All your bridesmaids should coordinate in as many ways as possible. They don't have to match like Rockettes, but you wouldn't want one of your bridesmaids to have an elaborate, upswept hairdo while the others wear their hair down in simple styles. Nor would you want one bridesmaid to wear red lipstick while the others are wearing pale, neutral colors. *All* the elements of your bridesmaids' ensembles should be considered soon after you've chosen their dresses and shoes.

All Together Now

I did a wedding recently where the bridesmaids ranged in age from twenty-five to thirty-five, and in size from a petite six to a twelve. The women all wore simple, elegant Nicole Miller evening dresses that cost under $250 each. The dresses looked perfect, but the bridesmaids all wore different shoes. That took away from the coordinated effect.

If you're going to have your bridesmaids all wear the same dress, you should have them wear the same shoes, too. And it should be the right shoes—evening shoes, simple pumps, or strappy, sexy cocktail shoes, in peau de soie, or any kind of textured material. Black leather shoes that you might wear with a suit to work are not appropriate for a wedding. Make sure that you select a heel height that all your bridesmaids will be comfortable in.

I also believe in coordinating jewelry and makeup among your bridesmaids. Attendants need not match the bride, but they should try to match one another.

There's a tradition of giving bridesmaids a gift, and it's nice if you give them something to wear on your wedding day. If you don't give them chiffon shawls, a necklace or earrings to wear to the wedding make a thoughtful gift. And this ensures that everyone is wearing the same accessories.

As for makeup, not everyone looks good in the same colors. But try to pick one or two colors of lipstick and eye shadow from the same family, so that the coordination will be carried through, right down to your bridesmaids' smiles. Buy these cosmetics and have them on hand for bridesmaids when they're dressing and applying makeup before the wedding. There's no sense leaving anything to chance.

Bridesmaid no-no's:

- Uncoordinated shoes
- Uncoordinated panty hose (sheer hose in the color family of the dress is most appropriate)
- Everyday jewelry
- Dark nail polish
- Glitzy evening makeup

Hair options

Your bridesmaids' hair should be in keeping with the formality and general style sensibility of your hair on your wedding day. Keeping in mind that most bridesmaids will not have a hairdresser to assist them in creating their hair the way that you might, spend time with each bridesmaid before the wedding day, deciding on style.

Following are some modern hair options that I recommend for bridesmaids. They're all very simple and elegant and will allow the bridesmaids to complement one another, and the bride.

The Man of the Hour . . . Grooming Your Groom

9

IN PLANNING A WEDDING, THERE IS SO MUCH THOUGHT given to the bride. The bride is the centerpiece of the wedding, even today when there's more equality in marriage. Everyone wants to know about the bride's dress and what she's going to look like. And the groom takes a bit of a backseat.

But while the groom might not call as much attention to himself, the way he looks on his wedding day is still really important. A nicely styled groom, who complements his bride's styling and cuts a confident, well-groomed image, can make all the difference to the overall picture. The groom, in effect, completes the picture.

When you are determining what you are going to look like, you should keep in mind what you want your groom to look like—and what you think he'll be comfortable in— before your project your image on him. If he's a jeans-and-T-shirt kind of guy, think about whether he's going to feel incredibly awkward in a really fancy tuxedo—or if he will enjoy the contrast from his everyday life. (A lot of grooms really get into dressing up for their wedding.)

Just as you wrote a paragraph about your vision for the wedding, you might want to write a paragraph about what you'd like to see your groom look like. It's also a good idea to make two checklists, one for your groom's outfit and the other for his grooming needs on the day of the wedding. For sample checklists, turn to the end of this chapter.

Well Suited

Depending on the time of year, the time of day, and the day of the week on which you're getting married, your groom has a number of clothing options. For an outdoor, Sunday-morning wedding, he can wear anything from tan pants and a blue blazer to a morning suit—depending on how formal the affair is (although morning suits can look costumey and overly dramatic if your groom isn't typically a very dressy dresser). He can wear a beautiful blue suit and great tie, even though you're wearing a formal wedding gown. The most popular choice still seems to be the tuxedo. But the most important thing is to make sure that his outfit coordinates with and complements yours—and that it fits him correctly.

❧ A tuxedo is the most standard clothing choice for a groom at his wedding. But if you are getting married in July or August, let's say in a warm place like Hawaii or Florida, your groom might look great in a cream or white classic suit, with a complementary vest in natural or khaki. His shirt should be either white, royal blue, or navy, although a blue shirt with any shade of khaki or cream suit can dress up a groom's ensemble. You could get a little more formal with your choice of a tie, going with a gray or silver with a black or a navy stripe. With this type of ensemble, your groom's shoes must be either white or natural buck.

There are other options, too, including pinstriped suits, black, brown, or navy suits—but these coordinate best with wedding gowns that aren't too fancy.

Otherwise, try to avoid having your groom wear a traditional business suit, or a tweed suit. Remember, this is a special day. Neither of you should too closely resemble your workaday selves.

❧ If your groom owns a tuxedo and assumes he can wear it for the wedding, take a good look at it. Is the fabric the right weight for the season? Is it out of style? Is it shiny from too many pressings? You may need to look farther than his closet.

The world of tuxedos is more vast than many people realize, with lots of different styles and varying degrees of formality. Classic styling is usually the best way to go—two- or three-button jackets with medium-sized lapels and no shoulder pads (except when advised by a tailor). Double-breasted tuxedos are good for stockier or heavier men, even though they also look great on tall, well-proportioned grooms. Just remember—double-breasted jackets don't usually get unbuttoned, so it might be a bit restricting to wear all through the wedding.

If your groom is as excited as you are to take the time and investigate his options, great! If not, you can pull off dressing him, too. Just bring your groom to a tux rental shop to be measured, and then you can do all the shopping on your own.

Even if your groom is very hands-on, you might want to explore this realm a little bit on your own first, before shopping with him. I recommend beginning your search in a fine department store.

A double-breasted tux looks best on a tall, broad-shouldered man. Shorter men should opt for two- or three-button jackets with medium-sized lapels.

At fine department stores you can check out the really expensive designer tuxedos, just to get an idea of style. Some tips: Hugo Boss makes a tux that fits broad-shouldered men of average height, five ten and taller, very well with great style; Giorgio Armani's tuxedos tend to be so slim in cut, with such small-shoulders, that his designs appeal primarily to shorter men. Sometimes a designer like Donna Karan will offer a slightly more unusual tuxedo, maybe with a tunic collar. But those exotic varieties are really best for men who might have a use for more than one tuxedo. It's important for all men to have a classic-styled tux in their wardrobe.

And, of course, also go to the tuxedo rental store. But keep in mind: A tuxedo is wrong if it looks rented.

❧ The same goes for his shoes. Those shiny rental shoes look plastic and rented, and even worse—they're very, very uncomfortable. I suggest that your groom get a beautiful pair of standard, black lace-up shoes, which he can wear again. Another nice option is black velvet slipper shoes, perhaps with a gold crest on the toe for a more formal affair.

❧ Of course, he'll need nice socks, too—not those thin, nylon socks but comfortable, black cotton ones, which go up his calf. He'll be crossing his legs and dancing, and his socks are going to show.

❧ As for shirts, if your groom is going to wear a tuxedo or a dinner jacket, I prefer white, 100 percent cotton styles. The days of ruffled-front shirts are long gone. Shirts with flat, sewn-down pleats are great. The collar is up to you. I prefer a stiff short-to-medium-length collar, or a wing tip with a black bow tie.

Even with a dark navy or black suit, I still prefer a white, 100 percent cotton shirt. In this case, you'd have him wear a really great necktie, perhaps from Giorgio Armani.

But there is something to be said about a blue shirt with a dark suit (so long as it's not a brown suit). It can look quite sharp. Match the blue shirt with a striking, almost bold tie, or even better, a blue tie that is just a shade darker or lighter than the shirt. Black suit, dark blue shirt, blue tie—this is a very modern, very chic tone-on-tone look.

❧ Most men wear cummerbunds with their tuxedos; but that isn't the only option, or necessarily the best-looking alternative. Ask your groom to consider wearing a vest instead, and maybe have him try some on. I prefer vests to cummerbunds. The look is more finished, and if he takes his jacket off during the reception, he will still appear to be well-dressed and together. A cummerbund tends not to stay in place nicely and ride up his back.

If you are buying a tux and a vest does not come with it, most department stores have a men's formal furnishings department where you can find vests, bow ties, pocket squares, cuff links, stays, and other accessories. If you buy a separate vest, make sure the material is at least a very close match to the tuxedo fabric. I think that vests should be black, to match the tuxedo. I'm not fond of vests in accent colors, like red or green. However, a white dinner jacket with a black vest, black pants, and black bow tie can look really sharp.

❧ Do you want your groom to wear a bow tie or a real tie, in either a bow or regular necktie fashion? In any case, DO NOT wait until the day of the wedding to figure out who can tie it. (Remember, even if you can tie it, that's no help, because you're going to be getting yourself ready.) Make sure there's someone in the wedding party who knows how to do this.

❧ The groom's other accessories and jewelry should be very subtle, so that he doesn't upstage the bride. If he wears an earring, it should be a simple post or stud. If he has long hair, perhaps suggest that he wear it in a covered ponytail band.

Here's a classic, vested tuxedo. When the jacket comes off, the vest ensures that your groom will still look neat and pulled together.

Grooming Your Groom

You certainly won't need anyone to remind you to get a manicure, have your hair done, and tend to all the other grooming procedures on your list before the wedding. But your groom might need some encouragement. Here's a quick summary of things you should remind your groom to do:

❧ Even if he doesn't normally wear a cotton undershirt, he should have one for the wedding, because he will perspire from nerves, dancing, and other activities.

❧ Do not let him get his hair cut the day before the wedding. A week before is much better, so that it will have grown into a natural look, and he'll have gotten comfortable with it.

❧ Make sure the hair on his neck and around his ears is cleaned up before the wedding day.

❧ See that his sideburns are even and his beard is trimmed properly. And bear in mind that men grow hair in strange places; watch out for ear and nose hairs, and make sure they're trimmed.

❧ Suggest that he get a manicure—and no, he doesn't have to wear polish.

❧ Have him go to the dentist for a cleaning and checkup.

❧ If he has a heavy beard and often cuts himself shaving, have him shave the night before the wedding instead of on the big day. The very last thing he should do before he goes to bed is take a shower in lukewarm water and shave. This way, the next morning when he wakes up, he's ready to go.

Another possibility is having him go for a barbershop shave. It's a fun activity for him to do with his groomsmen, the morning of the wedding. Your groom should try out a barbershop shave a week or two before the wedding, to make sure it's an experience he likes.

Groom's Checklist for Clothes and Accessories:

- Tux, rental or purchased, tailored and dry-cleaned
- Shirt pressed on a hanger
- Cuff links, buttons, shirt collars, and stays
- Tie and someone who knows how to tie it
- Wedding rings
- His own wristwatch
- Socks that match his ensemble (black socks with black tux)
- Shoes polished
- Belt
- White undershirt to prevent perspiration stains
- Groom and groomsmen lapel flowers

Groom's Checklist for Grooming:

- Neck hair and hair around the ears trimmed
- Manicure (polish is not necessary)
- Shaving (the night before if he has sensitive skin)
- Toothbrush and toothpaste for a quick pick-me-up before the wedding begins
- Handkerchief or tissues
- Deodorant

Give your groom his checklists once, about one month before the wedding, and again about two weeks before. Don't drive him crazy. If you're going to worry that he is not going to tend to everything on his list, then you are better off adding these things to your own list. But I'm sure your groom will surprise you. He has friends and family to face on the big day, too.

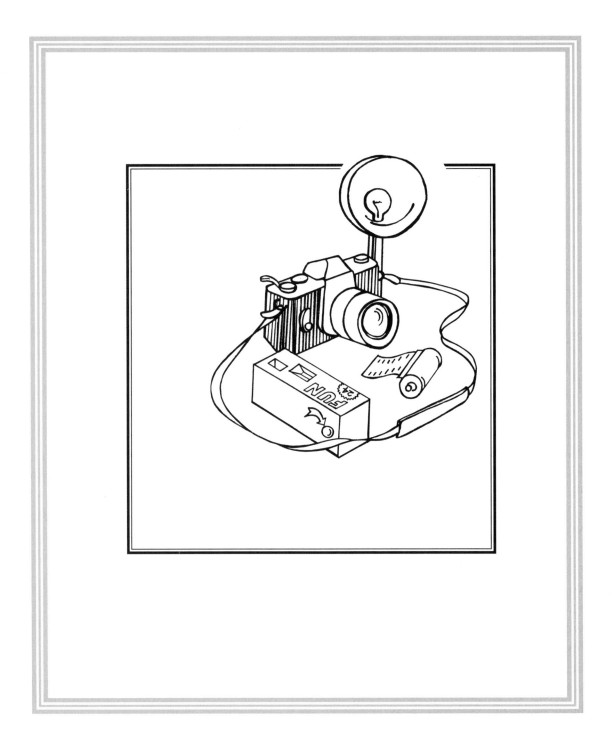

Picture Perfect . . . Capturing Your Wedding in the Perfect Light

10

T HEY SAY A PICTURE IS WORTH A THOUSAND WORDS. (Wedding photographers will tell you they're worth a few thousand dollars.) After your wedding, for years to come, there will be few things more valuable to you than your album of wedding photographs, and so it is really important to play an active role in making decisions about the photography—way ahead of time—so that you're happy with the final product.

There are many choices for you to make, from the photographer, to the color of the film, to the type of photographs you want to emphasize—traditional posed shots or candids— to the types of settings and lighting you want, and even at what point during the wedding you want your posed photographs to be taken. With all this to consider, it's best to begin thinking about your photography options as early as you can, probably as soon as your vision for the occasion begins to come into focus.

Before you even contact a photographer, you need to have some idea of what you're looking for. You need to have a sense of your concept, the style and tone of your wedding. It's even a good idea to have a notion of how many guests you'll have; there are some photographers, for instance, who won't do a wedding when there are more than two hundred guests.

Strike a Pose

The wedding photography realm has expanded a lot over the past few years as the bridal industry has grown, and different photographers tend to specialize in one type of photography or another.

The type of wedding you're having should help you to make the first choice—posed or candid, or a combination of the two. We're all familiar with the traditional, posed kind of photography, and it's still very popular, especially for more formal weddings. Traditional photography relies mainly on a variety of posed group shots, with the bride and groom appearing in many or most of them. Sometimes albums that contain only posed photos in this vein tend to seem a little stiff, and it's a good idea to also include some candids.

Less formal weddings lend themselves very well to candid photography. Actually, more and more brides these days are opting for candid photography, on the whole, or combined with posed shots. I have nothing against traditional wedding photography, but there's something very real and current about candid photographs.

Candid images also offer you a glimpse of the parts of the wedding that you were not present for. They capture your family and friends enjoying the wedding while you were having your first dance, or cutting the cake, or powdering your nose.

Take time to use your imagination and determine the general feel you want your wedding to have. Set up a few scenarios in your mind of your wedding day, with friends and family members, and imagine how you'd like moments like that captured on film. Then you will be better able to decide what type of photography you want and what type of photographer to hire.

Color Me Beautiful

Color film is still the traditional choice for wedding albums. There are benefits to color film, especially in summer months, when flowers are at their best and the sun shines brightly. In choosing whether to have all or some of your wedding photographs taken in color, you should consider the scenery at the place where you are to be married. If it's lush and vibrant, and warm enough to take pictures outdoors, color photography will work well.

Black-and-white film, however, is gaining in popularity, especially in urban areas. And there are advantages to black-and-white film, particularly during the winter months.

In general, everybody photographs better in black and white—it is much more forgiving than color. Every professional photographer knows that black-and-white film hides a thousand sins. It has a way of camouflaging wrinkles and blemishes, too. Black-and-white photography also provides more dramatic lighting options and can somehow make an event look timeless. That's an important issue to consider if you're planning to be a more modern or contemporary bride, and perhaps wear a trendier dress.

To give black-and-white photographs an even richer,

more timeless feeling, many brides choose to have them washed in what is called a sepia tone. This is a brownish or yellowish tint that can be applied to your prints—think of old family photographs from the earlier part of this century. Blue and pink tints are available, too. These options make for an interesting way to incorporate color into black-and-white photography.

On the other hand, one of the concerns with black-and-white film is that it can create some unwanted shadows. If, however, you look toward the light when you are photographed, you'll appear glowing and shadow-free.

Better Shop Around

Once you have a basic idea of the type and color of photography you want, it's time to start shopping around for a photographer. Knowing what you want, to some extent, will help you quickly rule out photographers who specialize in styles that don't appeal to you. You need to communicate your personal style, so that the photographers you speak to can let you know whether they can offer you the kinds of photos you're seeking. Otherwise, you might find your pictures will end up looking old-fashioned, stiff, or stodgy.

Right off the bat, you want to check out whether you are comfortable with each photographer you interview. This person is going to be a guest—albeit a hired one—at your wedding and will probably be the first to arrive and the last to leave. So it's important that you have a good rapport with him or her, that he or she will not be intrusive at your wedding, and will be willing to dress according to the code you choose.

Getting along fairly well with this person can enhance your wedding pictures, because it will affect your level of comfort and that of the other people in your wedding party. I've noticed that on professional photography shoots, if the photographer doesn't warm up to a model and boost her confidence, no matter how beautiful and natural that model is, she winds up looking stiff and uncomfortable.

Next, naturally, you want to take a look at their work. Here are some things to look for in the examples they show you:

- Is the lighting complementary? Or is it harsh and unflattering? You needn't be an expert to figure this out—it's a simple matter of opinion.
- Did the photographer use interesting backdrops? Did he or she take the best advantage of all the spaces available and the season?
- How many pictures include the backs of people's heads?
- Does it seem as if the family and wedding party were present in a majority of the photos? Or do the bride and groom appear to be conspicuously absent in most of the shots?

Once you're fairly sure you've found a photographer whose sensibilities match yours, and whom you like, it's a good idea to have him or her take an engagement photograph of you both before making the final decision. Engagement photographs were very popular years ago, and they're growing in popularity again. The engagement photo gives you two advantages: It's a way of documenting your engagement in a nice way, with pictures you can include in thank-you notes or display at the wedding; and it's a way of giving your photographer a final exam. It should be done at a relatively small expense.

Have a portrait done, in the studio or in natural light,

and have it printed in the color in which you expect to have your wedding photographs developed. Or, if you're still undecided, have it done in both black and white and color.

Once you've settled on a photographer, it's a good idea to provide him or her with Polaroids of the venue where you are to be married. Or, if possible, the photographer can go there to check out the lighting and the dimensions of the space.

A Friend in Deed

Not everyone hires a professional wedding photographer for their affair. It's becoming more and more common now to have family and friends take the pictures at a wedding. Especially since a lot of younger people prefer candid photographs these days, lots of brides and grooms are avoiding the huge expense of a wedding photographer by putting the task in the hands of someone close, who is either a professional photographer or who takes pictures as a hobby. That's a perfectly acceptable option, as long as you like their work and they're able to enjoy the wedding. And make sure you don't choose someone who has already been assigned other tasks—you don't want to have your very best friend be your maid of honor and the photographer. That's definitely not going to work.

No matter whom you choose, a friend or a hired professional, make sure that that person has an assistant with him or her the entire day. There is no photographer who can shoot an entire wedding solo and do a good job. An assistant serves many functions, including acting as a second pair of eyes to catch activity the photographer might miss while he or she is taking pictures, holding equipment and lights, and helping organize and fetch the right people for posed photographs.

Actually, you can put all your guests to work for some interesting candids by providing disposable cameras on each table at the wedding reception. It's pretty common for people to do that these days, and so most people know what to do when they see one of those cameras next to the bread basket. The result can be some of the best pictures of your guests taken that day.

Sitting Pretty

While most of the work regarding your pictures falls on the shoulders of the photographer, there are things that the bride should keep in mind, in order to get the best photographs and wedding album possible. Following are some suggestions:

❧ Whether you're using a hired professional or a friend as your wedding photographer, make sure she or he has either a big white card or a silver or white reflector. This can be the one tool that stands between you and great, flattering photographs. By placing this reflector or card on the floor in front of you, a photographer can manipulate the lighting to reduce the appearance of wrinkles, bags, and blemishes.

❧ Play in front of the mirror before your wedding to determine the ways in which you photograph best. Find your proverbial best side. Be aware of your body type. If you're a woman on the heavier side, there's no reason why you ever have to be straight-on to the camera. Practice posing at a three-quarter stance. Also decide which side your hair might be falling to, and on which side the groom will stand. Practice a variety of poses—without forgetting that you need to place your hands, legs, and feet nicely.

You'll need to sit in front of a mirror to see how difficult it is to position yourself so you look natural and come across well in your pictures. Pull your legs and feet to one side to lengthen and narrow your lines, and to appear more poised. Then, take a deep breath and relax your hands, placing one on top of the other. Every once in a while, just shake yourself out, from your neck, to your hands to your feet, to just loosen yourself up.

❧ Even when you are posing for the more classic posed pictures—and most brides choose to have at least some of these—try to lighten up and smile naturally. You might even want to contrast these pictures with some filled with children and laughter. These shots will add very real quality to your album. It's all about looking comfortable and having fun for the camera.

❧ Most wedding gowns tend to be fairly bulky, so any sitting pose will require great attention to posture. I don't mean for you to try to be stiff; but when you sit down, lift your shoulders and lengthen your torso from your waist.

❧ I often hear photographers telling both models and brides that they need to put their chin down a little bit lower than if they were just looking across the room and not having their picture taken. So, listen to the photographer—having your chin down makes for a more flattering portrait. Be aware of the height at which he or she is holding the camera.

❧ When considering backdrops for your photographs within the wedding hall, keep in mind your hair color. Contrast is really important in photography, and so if you've got really dark hair, you might not want to take photographs in a dark library with mahogany walls.

❧ Have a little pouch with a few makeup items—powder, lipstick, blush, Q-Tips, tissues, a small mirror—somewhere on the sidelines so that you can be touched up easily, if necessary. Maybe put one of your bridesmaids in charge of keeping track of it and making sure it's ready wherever you are during the wedding.

All in the Timing

Before your wedding day, it's important to determine when you want most of your photography done, especially the posed pictures.

There are advantages and disadvantages to having pictures taken before the ceremony. The greatest plus is that if the majority of your photography is out of the way by the time the wedding begins, you're freer to enjoy the wedding. If you do all your pictures before the ceremony, however, your groom will see you before you walk down the aisle, which many brides want to avoid. An alternative option is to take all the separate pictures before the ceremony and get the rest done afterward.

You must let your photographer know your plan. Pre-thinking all the group photographs way ahead of time is a good idea, too. Decide which individuals you want photographed together, and let a bridesmaid and the photographer be aware of your plan—give them lists.

It's fun to have the photographer on the scene really early taking candids, while you're getting ready. The best shots happen when you're indisposed. Part of the fun of getting married is all the preparation, and you'll want to remember that part of it. I find myself witnessing these great behind-the-scenes moments all the time. I'll arrive early to meet with a bride, and usually within forty-five minutes, the female contingency of the wedding party starts to arrive. Before you know it, it's me and six to ten women. The adrenaline is flowing, and the excitement of the day begins here. The photographer should be catching every bit of this.

The White Album

The photographer, or your friend, has shot the wedding. Now, who makes the album? Who gets to keep the negatives? How many prints do you get—and do you have to keep paying the same photographer for more of them?

These are things you should know up front, if you're hiring a professional. One of the options may be that you get to keep the negatives if you make your own album.

While many brides opt to have the whole thing taken care of professionally, more and more women are making their own albums. There are lots of ready-made albums that have slots for you to insert the pictures yourself—and they're not just those pull-back plastic kind that you use for your vacation photos. They're more elaborate and elegant. Doing your own wedding album is the less expensive alternative, and it's a terrific option, because it gives you a chance to complete that last element of the wedding and still express your own style vision.

Don't-Forget List

11

I<small>N THE FINAL DAYS LEADING UP TO YOUR WEDDING,</small> there will be a number of things that you'll need to take care of to make sure everything goes smoothly—and to avoid some common calamities. I've put together a helpful list of some of the essentials you should have on hand for your wedding day. It's a time when you'll be the most frazzled, but try to stay calm and organized. Use this list as a guide, add any other items you can think of, and everything should be fine.

1. Underwear

You'll be wearing different underwear than you're used to for your wedding, probably a bra that works with your dress—like a strapless, backless style—and a pair of panties that shape you. So many brides arrive at the place where they're getting married in their regular clothes and under-

wear and forget to bring along their special undergarments. Then Dad has to run home and get the bra. *Don't* let this happen to you.

2. *Panty Hose*

The hose that will be appropriate for your wedding will be either white, off-white, or sheer. If your dress is one of the darker shades of cream, you can think about wearing neutral sheer hose. But whatever color you choose, be sure to buy a second—even a third—pair to have on hand on your wedding day, especially if you're prone to tearing your stockings in regular, everyday life. Keep in mind that you probably should purchase hose that have a sandal foot whether or not you're wearing open-toed shoes. If you want to slip your shoes off at any time during the reception, or if your feet hurt, you don't want to have that thick seam showing.

3. *Shoes*

Even if you've decided to purchase only one pair of special wedding shoes, and they're comfortable, you may just want to have an extra, inexpensive pair with you. There might be weather issues if there are any outdoor elements to your wedding. Also, you might spill something (a drink, makeup) on your shoes early in the day—or for some reason they might become uncomfortable over the course of the day. It never hurts to be prepared.

4. *Clothes to Wear Following the Wedding*

Once your wedding has ended, where do you go next? Will there be another party somewhere after the reception? Will you go out with friends and continue the celebrations? Are you hopping right on a plane, to head for your honeymoon? You should think about these possibilities ahead of time and pack a bag of whatever it is you might want to wear, whether it's your favorite old jeans or another dress. And don't forget to pack everyday underwear.

5. *Miscellaneous Grooming and Convenience Items*

You'll want to make sure the following items are available and on hand at the place where your wedding will be held:

- steamer
- hangers
- chairs
- mirror
- electricity
- a room for bridesmaids for changing
- air conditioning
- daylight

6. *Jewelry*

The night before your wedding, gather whatever jewelry you've decided to wear on your wedding day, and put it with everything else you'll be bringing with you.

7. *Fragrance*

Think ahead about whether you'll want to wear perfume, scented body powder, or lotion. Pack these essentials the night before.

8. *Other Toiletries*

You may want to pack a toiletry bag with some basics. Pack as if you're going somewhere overnight, and include a toothbrush, toothpaste, Q-Tips, deodorant, and anything else you use regularly. You're going to be getting dressed at a place away from home, so you'll need your regular grooming products.

9. *Golf Umbrella*

If you are concerned about the weather, it's a good idea to have a nice big golf umbrella or two in the car so that when you get in and out, your hair and clothes won't get ruined.

10. *Wedding Day Makeup Pouch*

In the makeup chapter of this book, I talk about a discreet little pouch that you should have handy on your wedding day. Make sure that one of your bridesmaids can easily find it for you, so that you can touch up your hair and makeup whenever you need to. Here's a recap of what this pouch should contain:

- tissues
- lipsticks
- bobby pins
- hairbrush or comb
- handkerchief
- Q-Tips
- face powder
- breath spray
- a tiny hair spray sample

➤ white-out (there's nothing better for stains on a white dress!)

11. Groom's Checklist

See the more complete groom's checklist at the end of the groom chapter. Be sure to remind him to make sure he has the following items in order and ready for the wedding day:

➤ tie
➤ shirt
➤ cuff links
➤ shirt stays
➤ studs
➤ dark socks
➤ suit or tux
➤ shoes

12. Clear Nail Polish

This is a staple item in every bride's emergency kit. Clear nail polish will fix the run in your (and your bridesmaids') panty hose. And you also can use it to touch up your manicure if necessary.

13. Needle and Thread

What if your groom loses a button on his shirt? Or, worse yet, what if one of the tiny buttons or rosettes on your dress falls off while you are dressing? A needle and thread will save you in a pinch. Tuck away one of those traveler's sewing kits in your toiletry bag. You won't regret it.

I've put together this sample countdown calender to help you budget your time efficiently for the month leading up to your wedding. It's filled with good suggestions and reminders to help make that homestretch not only less hectic but also more fun. I've included a blank calender, too, so that you can organize your own schedule. Feel free to scribble right on these pages. Don't forget—be realistic and leave plenty of time for all the practice runs, errands, and grooming considerations.

Last Month Countdown Before the Wedding...
A Helpful Monthlong Calendar

1	2	3	4	5	6	7
• Facial/ Dermatologist • Pick up headpiece	• Last fitting • Pick up dress	• First hair try	• Buy lipstick for bridesmaids, maybe eye shadow	• First makeup try	• First practice of walking in shoes	
8	**9**	**10**	**11**	**12**	**13**	**14**
	• Walk in shoes with flowers and headpiece (keep head up)	• Bang trim • Walk in shoes	• Timed hair and makeup try		• Teeth cleaning	• Wedding shower
15	**16**	**17**	**18**	**19**	**20**	**21**
		• Touch up hair color		• Final dress rehearsal at home with hair and makeup	• Call to florist to confirm personal and wedding flowers	• Call to confirm clothes for groom and best man
22	**23**	**24**	**25**	**26**	**27**	**28**
• Pay all bills before leaving for honeymoon	• Pick up and inspect the groom's clothes	• Start packing for honeymoon	• Pick up dry cleaning • All waxing (eyebrows, bikini, legs)	• Manicure and pedicure • Finishing packing • Scan don't-forget list	• Blow-dry hair straight REHEARSAL DINNER	**WEDDING DAY** Good Luck!
29	**30**	**31**				
Next day brunch	Beginning of the honeymoon					

Personal Countdown

1	2	3	4	5	6	7
8	9	10	11	12	13	14
15	16	17	18	19	20	21
22	23	24	25	26	27	28
29	30	31				

Dear Reader,

As you reach this final page, I hope you have made some decisions about how you want to set the tone for style and beauty at your wedding. It is my wish that the experiences I've shared in *The Beautiful Bride* helped boost your confidence in your choices and allowed you to follow your instincts. It might be a good idea to hang on to the book right up until the last minute, rereading chapters if necessary, taking notes in the margins. This book is meant to be your security blanket. You might even want to pass it along—with your notes in it—to a friend or relative, or whoever catches the bouquet. Just remember how much easier it can all be when you have this book at your side.

Writing this guide has been an opportunity for me to reminisce about all the beautiful brides I've worked with over the course of the last few years. I love weddings. I wish I could be there with each and every one of you. But since I can't, the anecdotes I've included will help you realize you're not alone in your worries, concerns, and dreams for a beautiful wedding.

It's my greatest hope that *The Beautiful Bride* provided you with a positive planning experience that will be a springboard for a happy marriage and life. Good luck!

Mitchell Behr

Resources

Bride and Bridesmaid Dresses
These are a few terrific boutiques, bridal stores, and veritable bridal emporiums in selected cities across the nation that carry a wide selection of bride and bridesmaid dresses. Check local listings for telephone numbers and exact locations.

California
The Wedding Dress at Saks Fifth Ave.—Beverly Hills
Alley—Los Angeles
Mon Amie—Costa Mesa

Florida
Formal Threads—Boca Raton
Davenports—Jacksonville

Georgia
The Wedding Dress at Saks Fifth Ave.—Atlanta
Belles & Beaus—Fayetteville

Illinois
House of Brides—Chicago
Exclusive for Brides—Chicago

New York
Kleinfelds—Brooklyn
Bergdorf Goodman—New York City

Texas
Patsy's—Dallas
Neiman Marcus—Dallas

Dress Designers
Following are listings of some of my favorite designers mentioned in the book, plus retail outlets that carry their labels. These designers create traditional bridal gowns as well as elegant evening dresses that work well as bridal gowns.

Vera Wang—(212) 628–3400
    Vera Wang Bridal Salon at Barney's—New York, NY;
        Beverly Hills, CA
    Vera Wang Bridal House—New York, NY
    Suky Rosan—Ardome, PA
    Jingles—Richmond, VA
    Formal Threads—Boca Raton, FL
    Exclusively for Brides—Chicago, IL

Morgan Le Fay—(212) 879–9700
    Bergdorf Goodman—New York, NY

Morgan Le Fay Boutique in Soho and Madison Avenue—New York, NY
Morgan Le Fay Boutique—Santa Monica, CA

Ilissa—(212) 967-5222
Aluins—Birmingham, MI
Alegrias—Coral Gables, FL
Brides by Roma—Paramus, NJ
Bridal and Formal—Cincinnati, OH
Mon Amie—Costa Mesa, CA

Galina—(212) 564-1020
Patsy's—Dallas, TX
Clarissa—Walnut Creek, CA
Bridal Reflections—Massapequa, NY
Suky Rosan—Ardome, PA
Exclusively for Brides—Chicago, IL

Bill Levkoff—(888) 583-5633
Call for a store in your area.

Shopping Reference for Veil and Headpiece

Wedding Belles
Marina Biagioli & Marie Butchen
2848 Long Beach Road
Oceanside, NY 11572
(516) 764-1390

These talented women have been designing and manufacturing custom-made veils and headpieces forever. They can custom-design a veil and headpiece based on your ideas, or you can purchase ready-made veils and headpieces from them.

Or just give them a call for great advice on how to accessorize your dress.

Shoes
Look for these labels when shopping for the perfect pair of
wedding shoes.

Peter Fox—(212) 744–8340
> Available in Peter Fox Stores in New York, California,
> and Toronto.

Manolo Blahnik—(212) 582–3007
> New York—Bergdorf Goodman, Saks Fifth Ave.,
>   Bloomingdale's, Neiman Marcus, and Barney's
> California—Neiman Marcus and Barney's
> Illinois—Neiman Marcus and Saks Fifth Ave.
> Florida—Dillard's and Burdine's
> Georgia—Neiman Marcus
> Texas: Dillard's and Neiman Marcus

Stuart Weitzman—(212) 582–9500
> New York—Bergdorf Goodman, Saks Fifth Ave.,
>   Bloomingdale's, Neiman Marcus, and Macy's
> California—Neiman Marcus and Nordstrom's
> Illinois—Neiman Marcus and Saks Fifth Ave.
> Florida—Dillard's and Burdine's
> Georgia—Neiman Marcus
> Texas—Dillard's and Neiman Marcus

Nine West—(800) 260–2227
Call for the location of the Nine West store nearest you.
> New York—Bloomingdale's, Macy's, Neiman Marcus,
>   Filene's Basement

California—Nordstrom's, Macy's, Burdine's
Florida—Burdine's and Dillard's
Illinois—Saks Fifth Ave. and Neiman Marcus

Kenneth Cole—(800) KEN-COLE
Call for the location of the Kenneth Cole store nearest you.
New York—Lord & Taylor, Macy's, and Bloomingdale's
Florida—Burdine's
California—Neiman Marcus and Nordstrom's
Georgia—Neiman Marcus and Nordstrom's
Texas—Neiman Marcus, Nordstrom's, and Burdine's

Tuxedos

When your groom is ready to shop for a tuxedo, encourage him to check out the following labels. Better yet, make sure you accompany him on his shopping mission.

Giorgio Armani—(212) 988–9191
Call for the location of a store carrying Armani near you.
New York—Bergdorf Goodman, Saks Fifth Ave., Neiman Marcus
Illinois—Saks Fifth Ave. and Neiman Marcus
Georgia—Neiman Marcus
Florida—Neiman Marcus
Texas—Neiman Marcus
California—Neiman Marcus

Hugo Boss—(212) 940–0600
New York—Bergdorf Goodman, Macy's, Bloomingdale's, Saks Fifth Ave., Neiman Marcus
Florida—Burdine's, Dillard's, Surry's, Neiman Marcus
Georgia—Neiman Marcus

California—Macy's and Neiman Marcus
Illinois—Neiman Marcus and Saks Fifth Ave.
Texas—Neiman Marcus and Dillard's

Donna Karan—(800) 231–0884
New York—Saks Fifth Ave., Bergdorf Goodman, Barney's, Neiman Marcus
California—Neiman Marcus
Georgia—Neiman Marcus
Texas—Neiman Marcus
Illinois—Saks Fifth Ave. and Neiman Marcus

Behr Naked is Mitchell Behr's full line of makeup and hair-care products. These products are available through direct mail.

Write or call for a catalog or speak with a Behr Naked representative:

Behr Naked
17 Glade Road
East Hampton, NY 11937
Tel: (516) 324–3580

The Beautiful Bride Makeup Kit, a special product offered by Behr Naked, includes:

- Oil-free or whipped foundation
- Loose powder
- 1 eyebrow pencil
- 5 eyeshadow colors
- 2 blushes
- 1 lip pencil
- 2 lipsticks
- 5 makeup brushes
- Mascara

AND

- Step-by-step application cards

The cost for the kit is $150, plus shipping and handling. Products are returnable unopened. Freight return paid by customer.

About the Author

Mitchell Behr is a New York City–based bridal style specialist, makeup and hair stylist, and image consultant. In addition to his private bridal consulting, his bridal editorial work has appeared in *Condé Nast Brides*.

An image consultant for recording artists in the music industry, Mitchell also has been a hair and makeup stylist for several music videos. He is Style Director for *The Mark and Kathy Show* on TBS and has worked on national advertising campaigns for Sears, Avon, Levi's, and Structure. His general editorial work has been featured in *Marie Claire, YM, Women's Wear Daily, Papier,* the *San Francisco Examiner,* and *Raygun.*

OTHER BOOKS OF INTEREST

BRIDAL SHOWERS

by Sharon E. Dlugosch and Florence E. Nelson
0-399-51344-2/$10.00

A total how-to handbook for friends and family of the bride-to-be. *A Perigee Trade Paperback*

BRIDE'S ALL-NEW BOOK OF ETIQUETTE

by the editors of *Bride's* magazine 0-399-51834-7/$16.95

With more than 500,000 copies sold, this wedding-planning classic has been completely revised and updated for the nineties. *A Perigee Trade Paperback*

BRIDE'S NEW WAYS TO WED

by the editors of *Bride's* magazine and Antonia Van der Meer 0-399-51575-5/$9.95

From *Bride's* magazine, the most trusted source for wedding information, here is a complete wedding planner for a truly personalized wedding. *A Perigee Trade Paperback*

BRIDE'S SHORTCUTS AND STRATEGIES FOR A BEAUTIFUL WEDDING

by the editors of *Bride's* magazine and Kathy C. Mullins 0-399-51224-1/$8.95

The indispensable guide to planning a beautiful wedding in only a few weeks or a few months. With many time-saving tips and more. *A Perigee Trade Paperback*

HOW TO HAVE THE WEDDING YOU WANT
(NOT THE ONE EVERYBODY ELSE WANTS YOU TO HAVE)

by Danielle Claro 0-425-14578-6/$12.00

Enthusiastic advice for the bride who desires an untraditional and creative wedding. *A Berkley Trade Paperback*